The Concept
of
Self

The Concept

of

Self

Kenneth J. Gergen

Swarthmore College

HOLT, RINEHART AND WINSTON, INC.
New York   Chicago   San Francisco   Atlanta
Dallas   Montreal   Toronto   London   Sydney

To Maria at Adriana

PREFACE

Of all the topics that draw students to the study of human behavior none is more compelling than self-interest. Human motivation is basically narcissistic, and self-understanding is a major means of avoiding pain and achieving pleasure. We have all heard the voices, "I wonder why I said that," "I just don't know why she doesn't like me," "I just can't seem to get myself going," "How can you love me with all my faults," "This just doesn't feel like the real me," and "I feel so wretched about myself that I just don't care anymore." In each of the voices the pivotal concern with "self" is clear. To understand who one is may provide answers to why one is loved or hated, why one succeeds or fails, why one feels whole and intact or fragmented and artificial, and so on.

The quest for self-understanding is usually a haphazard one—a glimpse of "reality" emerges here, a sudden insight occurs there, and in between the person stumbles through the disconnected and ambiguous events of daily life. In part this occurs because he is not trained to observe; he is unsystematic and does not utilize the appropriate tools. The present volume attempts to furnish the means for better self-understanding. It will provide concepts with which the flux can hopefully be rendered more coherent; it will provide arguments about the nature of "self" that are often grounded in empirical evidence. And it will point to critical issues in the process of self-understanding that should focus the search and increase its yield for the individual.

But lest I mislead, the emphasis of this book is not on the "self" as much as it is on the process of self-understanding. The reader must carry with him through the pages the baggage of his own memories. If the book is to have an impact, the reader must open himself to its implications for his own life. For rather than concentrating on the personal experiences of the reader, the volume will center on the process by which the individual copes with these experiences. In the final analysis, one's personal conduct is based upon his conception of "reality" rather than upon reality itself. And it is the *process* of self-understanding that is more important than the "self" which the individual attempts to understand. The "self" may always elude our comprehension, but the process of comprehension is open to understanding.

All the ideas within this book have been sharpened and vitalized by my wife Mary. Chad Gordon and Stan Morse have also contributed greatly to the quality of the final product. And in the later stages, both Susan Terdiman and Marilyn Wade provided much needed assistance with the manuscript.

K. J. G.

Swarthmore, Pennsylvania
November 1970

CONTENTS

ix

x   Contents

The Concept of Self

I

The Study of Self

THE FOLLOWING NOTE WAS RECENTLY RECEIVED from a young research assistant:

> It looks as if global self-evaluations like self-esteem might have been affected unconsciously by the total picture presented by the other in the salient condition.
> I'm so excited, I can't stop jumping around!

How, you might ask, can such abstract double-talk motivate this excitement? Why does the assistant consider such a topic worthwhile? Why should investigators be drawn to the study of self—to the study of a person's notions of who or what he is?

The prominent role of self-psychology can be largely attributed to the *human* side of the scientific enterprise. Behavioral scientists are products of their cultural heritage before they are scientists. In the quest for rigor many have attempted to cast off this background, believing the values and sentiments reflected in their heritage to be biases that may blind them to objective fact. The self-psychologist, however, is less concerned with cutting himself away from his past. For him the human concern with self that has recurred for century after century furnishes a major challenge for contemporary science.

A person's concern with who he is has ancient roots indeed, and takes many forms. What are some of the ways in which the self has occupied man's thought and feelings? In a broad sense this is to ask why the self is considered an important object of psychological study and what questions might be put to scientific investigation today. Four concerns are especially apparent.

The first of these concerns has persisted from the time of the early Greeks to the present day and relates to man's knowledge of who he is— his *identity*. This concern is reflected in the ancient dictum, "Know thyself." Plutarch noted that this inscription had been carved on the Delphic oracle, that mystical sanctuary where kings and generals sought advice on matters of greatest importance to them. The statement has variously been attributed to Plato, Pythagoras, Thales, and Socrates, and the early Roman poet Juvenal went so far as to say that the precept descended from Heaven. In later times blood was shed over the issue of man's identity. Christendom could little tolerate a redefinition of man as less than the center of Creation, as no more than an animal. Today we find theorists in the field of mental health arguing that a sense of identity is far more crucial for mental well-being than any concept defined in the Freudian tradition.

Why has the problem of man's identity been so important to so many? A volume could be devoted to this topic alone, but it is sufficient to say here that the way in which a man conceives of himself will influence both what he chooses to do and what he expects from life. If one believes himself to be a great sinner, he may spend a lifetime in repentance; if he feels himself to be an agent free of social constraint, like Dostoevsky's Raskolnikov, he may become a murderer; if he feels himself to be a victim of "the establishment," he may take to the barricades. For one to know his identity, then, is to grasp the meaning of his past and his potential for the future.

Second, and equally important to the problem of self-definition, is man's concern with *self-evaluation*. What feelings should a man have about himself; how should he value himself? This issue has occasioned centuries of debate. On the one hand we find those who denounce self-love, holding it to be a major flaw in character, a point of view which is integral to the Judaeo-Christian tradition. The Book of Proverbs contains many admonitions against self-love, such as "Pride goeth before destruction, and a haughty spirit before a fall." And later we find Thomas Moore echoing this sentiment with, "Humility, that low, sweet root/From which all heavenly virtues shoot." However, railing against vanity is hardly limited to the religious. In the early 1700s the satirist Alexander Pope wrote:

> Of all the causes which conspire to blind
> Man's erring judgment, and misguide the mind,
> What the weak head and the strongest bias rules,
> Is pride, the never-failing vice of fools.

At the same time, history has seen many champions of self-love. In early Roman times, the emperor Marcus Aurelius counseled, "Never esteem anything as of advantage . . . to thee that shall make thee . . . lose thy respect of self." Christian humility must have indeed seemed alien and loathsome to the Roman leaders who gloried in self-aggrandizement. The Emperor Nero, for instance, had erected in the vestibule of his home a bronze statue of himself, 120 feet high. In the 1600s John Milton took up the banner, writing, "Oft times nothing profits more than self-esteem, grounded on just and right." Two hundred years later Alfred Lord Tennyson added, "Self-reverence, self-knowledge, self-control, these three alone lead life to sovereign power." And in the twentieth century the poet Helene Mullins adds:

> Only the stern self-confident can hold
> Their peace amidst the clamor, nor betray
> Their capabilities; can sit unmoved,
> With all around them trembling to have told
> The utmost of their merits; only they
> Can bear to leave their strength unguessed, unproved.

In present-day psychology the question of "how much self-love" continues to be a central one. The majority of thinking on this subject runs counter to the Judaeo-Christian tradition. From the point of view of mental health and human happiness, a significant degree of self-love seems a necessity.

A third major issue can be traced to the long-standing feeling of basic conflict between *self* and *society*. From one point of view, the self is treated as a set of core feelings or perceptions the person has about himself which demand reverence because they uniquely distinguish the individual from others. Society, in this view, is seen as a *bête noire* in its continued intrusiveness and in the compromises it demands of the "true self." Such sentiments appear as early as 42 B.C. with Publilius Syrus' maxim, "It matters not what you are thought to be, but what you are." Perhaps the most often quoted statement in support of self-integrity is Polonious' advice in the Hamlet tradegy, "To thine own self be true, and it must follow as the night the day, thou canst not then be false to any man." The British poet, Richard Francis Burton, may have been influenced by Shakespeare when he wrote, "He noblest lives and noblest dies who makes and keeps his self-made laws." We also find embodied in Latin form on the North Carolina state seal the sentiment, "To be, rather than to seem."

But in spite of the widespread commitment to self-integrity, there are many who have felt that such a commitment is an encumbrance. In this case the world is seen as a place where multiple rewards are available to those who are flexible and where disaster falls to those with a romantic commitment to an intractable identity. Perhaps we are viewing flexibility in action when we find Publilius Syrus contradicting his early support for self-integrity with the maxim, "It is sometimes better to forget who we are." Machiavelli elaborated on this theme some 15 centuries later with his emphasis on deception and on the management of self-appearance for political ends. More recently the psychiatrist Emil Ludwig has argued that telling small lies about oneself may be vitally necessary for the happiness of others—and thus, indirectly, for one's own happiness. And certainly there is merit in the position that to be inflexible is to be maladaptive. But can we jettison the notion of self-integrity? Just how beneficial is it to behave in ways that contradict what one feels he is? As we go on, we shall formulate this problem in such a way that factual answers can be reached.

A fourth issue will round out our discussion. Over the years many have been concerned with the self, not for its positive value but for the *restrictions* and *limitations* it imposes. The British author William Hazlitt saw the self as interfering primarily with lusty spontaneity: "Oh! it is great to shake off the trammels of the world . . . to lose our importunate, tormenting, everlasting personal identity and become the creature of the moment." Nathaniel Hawthorne phrased this concern with self as an impediment most dramatically, "What other dungeon is so dark as one's own heart! What jailer as inexorable as one's self?" More recently, the contemporary German author Herman Hesse has dealt at length with the problems involved in shedding one's timeworn conceptions of self. The protagonist in *Steppenwolf* undergoes a tortuous internal journey, discovering wellsprings of potential hidden beneath the identity so familiar to him. How can we understand these poetic sentiments in a more formal sense? Can a scientific approach lend itself to dealing with this subjective concern?

These are only a few of the issues that have seeded thinking and research on the self. Many have come to investigate the self out of a practical interest in mental health. In dealing with psychosis, we find numerous instances in which an identity transformation has seemingly resulted from the pain of an earlier identity. To fancy oneself as Napoleon, for instance, may allow one to feel omnipotent in a world that otherwise appears devoid of choice. To become Jesus Christ may allow one to believe that he is blessed by God when those around him have "crucified" him in subtle ways. But the importance of the self is hardly limited to the domain of severe disturbance. Many day-to-day problems are also intimately connected to self-perception. One person is depressed because he perceives that he has no worth or that he fails to merit the love of others. Another may feel anxious because he does not seem to be *anyone* in particular, just a reflection of those about him. And still others may undergo a peculiar sense of dread when they see themselves as a small finite speck in an irrational cosmos.

In addition to its relevance to the areas of health and adjustment, the self is often viewed as a vital factor in understanding human social behavior. Social psychologists have long been concerned with building laws that explain interaction between people. Primarily, the attempt has been to use as few theoretical terms as possible in building such principles, quite in keeping with the philosophically sound policy of parsimony. However, in spite of the effort to keep explanatory factors to a minimum, these principles have continuously proven to be much more accurate, more precise in what they predict, when the person's definition of self is taken into account.

As one example of this increased power of prediction, there is the belief that the civil rights movement places pressure on the young Negro to commit himself behaviorally—to take public action. And while this pressure is generally successful, there are numerous exceptions. Thousands of Negroes who share the liberal ideology do not participate in demonstrations or other forms of protest. Gore and Rotter (1963) carried out a study attempting to find out what caused such differences in participation level. It was found that the individual's perception of his control over his environment was central. Those who saw themselves as independent of environmental forces and in control of their lives and what happened to them frequently participated in civil rights activities. Those who believed they were pawns at the mercy of the powers that be were much less active. Self-definition, then, was all important in predicting civil rights activity.

For these and other reasons the topic of self has compelled widespread attention. It should be recognized, however, that the study of self has not always been welcome in the scientific realm. It will be to our advantage now to examine briefly the history of the study of self.

SELF-STUDY: HISTORY IN BRIEF

Any detailed account of thinking on the self would certainly trace its origins to early Greek writings. The distinction made by Aristotle and others between the physical and nonphysical aspects of the human being came to play a mammoth role in the study of human functioning. One central concept of nonphysical existence was *soul*. The meaning of this term was never very precise in early thought; often it was used to refer to the *core* of the nonphysical or psychic, that part which is essential and unique in mental functioning. This notion has much in common with what later theorists meant by "self." With the advent of Christianity, however, the concept of soul became the property of theology, and its relevance to scientific thinking became increasingly remote.

Aristotle's basic distinction between the physical and nonphysical aspects of human functioning continued to prevail, however, and some 2000 years later it was elaborated further by the French philosopher René Descartes. Although Descartes had much to say about the relationship between body and mind, it was the reasoning underlying his celebrated dictum "I think, therefore I am," that challenged thinkers for centuries to come. Essentially, Descartes reasoned that since the reality of *thinking* was undeniable, so was the existence of the thinker, or the *I*. This notion of *I*, the thinking, knowing, cognizing entity became one direct predecessor of the concept of self in psychology.

Problems such as the distinction between mind and body, understanding the existence of mind, the nature of human experience, and the nature of experiencing oneself became central to later philosophical thinking. Philosophers such as Berkeley, Hobbes, Hume, and James and John Stuart Mill were notable in the sophistication with which they examined such problems. It was out of this philosophical tradition that the field of psychology grew in the late 1800s. We shall have a chance to view some of these debates at closer range in Part II of this volume.

Early psychology was largely a psychology of personal experience. Using the method of introspection, the individual subject attempted to examine and report on his state of consciousness. It was also clear to many investigators that among the most important contents of the conscious mind were the individual's experiences of himself. For the early experimentalist Wilhelm Wundt, among others, the notion of self largely referred to the person's experience of his own body—self-feeling or self-awareness was primarily awareness of muscle tension or other internal states. However, with the rich and compelling theorizing of William James at the turn of the twentieth century, this restricted view was abandoned.

For James, the bodily self was subsumed under one of three categories of self-experience, the *Material Me*. James argued that a person experiences as his own material possession not only his body, but also his home, his family, and the physical objects with which he surrounds himself. A second category of self-experience fell under the heading of *Social Me*. Here was included the individual's awareness of his reputation or his identity in the eyes of others. For James, the person's awareness of himself as he feels others see him was just as real as muscle tension. The third category, the *Spiritual Me,* was more vague, but generally it referred to the individual's awareness of his own mental process—his thinking and feeling. It is interesting to note in connection with our earlier discussion of soul James' statement that, "This sense of [mental] activity is often held to be a direct revelation of the living substance of our Soul" (1892).

After James, the notion of self continued to grow in importance for some three decades, with a number of notable contributors to its development. Among the earliest was the sociologist Charles Horton Cooley, whose book *Human Nature and the Social Order* strongly emphasized the relationship between self and social environment. For Cooley, the person's feelings about himself were seen largely as products of his relations with others, relations that affected him from the early years of life, on. This view was later expanded in the influential writings of George Herbert Mead, who demonstrated the power of combining philosophical, psychological, and sociological perspectives. As we shall find in Part III, particularly challenging was Mead's discussion of the process by which the person's identity comes to reflect the views of those around him. For Mead, the person's view of self is a product of the social environment. The work of both Mead and Cooley are basic to what has been termed the *symbolic interactionist* orientation in sociology, an orientation that lays stress on psychological meaning in human relations. From this standpoint the concept of self is often viewed as the major link between the fields of sociology and psychology.

Freud's psychoanalytic theory also contributed to the widespread concern with self. The concept of *ego* in Freudian theory had much in common with the notion of self as viewed by a number of other theorists. For one thing, in psychoanalytic theory conscious awareness was largely subsumed under the concept of ego. Thus, the mechanisms of defense, the relationship of consciousness to the external world, the inculcation of moral values—all of which figure so prominently in Freudian theory— became topics of interest for the self-theorist. It remained for Freud's disciples, however, to extend psychoanalytic theory in ways most useful to later research on the self.

Most outstanding among those who followed Freud were Erich Fromm, Karen Horney, and Harry Stack Sullivan. Both Fromm and Horney made particularly important contributions to our understanding of self-love, the former emphasizing its importance for human happiness and the latter centering on neurotic forms of self-love. Horney also made seminal contributions to our knowledge of self-alienation—the person's feelings of estrangement from his "true self." This topic will receive special attention in Part IV. Sullivan, on the other hand, took a close look at the development of self during infancy, showing how feelings about self might rely on bodily pleasure or pain and how these bodily states depend on the treatment given the infant by its mother (as in breast feeding).

Early contributions came from other schools of thought as well. From James Mark Baldwin, the early developmental psychologist, came stimulating ideas on the function of imitation in developing self-consciousness. For him, the imitation of others was a major way of learning about oneself. He also theorized about ways in which one's view of self could influence his view of others. The way in which self-perception affects our perception of others will receive attention in Part IV.

The Gestalt school of perception furnished additional ideas concerning the way in which innate physiological processes might influence self-perception. This approach provided one way of understanding why people perceive a separation between themselves and others—a separation that seems, after all, an arbitrary one.[1] The esteemed social psychologist Kurt Lewin concentrated on the issue of ethnic identity and the problem of self-hatred among the Jews. In doing so he demonstrated the possibility of ultimately linking a theory of self with formal mathematics.

Such growth and ferment did not continue. During the 1920s the positivistic spirit began to prevail and, with its extreme emphasis on observable fact and thorough criticism of "armchair" theorizing, the status of self-theory began to wane. The positivistic orientation, inseparable from early behaviorism, was propounded and developed in psychology by Watson, Thorndike, Hull, and Skinner, to name but a few. Positivism was extremely attractive from several standpoints. It demonstrated the weakness of theory not tied to demonstrable fact. If theoretical concepts could not be linked to the empirical world, they must be dropped from scientific consideration; if a theory was not capable of being tested, the theory had no place in the domain of psychology. In this way, it was felt, psychology could truly take its place as a science, rather than remaining a handmaiden to philosophy.

Self-psychology was at that time quite vulnerable to such attacks. As we have already seen, there were multiple and often very ambiguous meanings for the term "self." Theoretical hairsplitting had been rampant from the beginning of self-study in psychology. Experimentation was also greatly lacking, and the introspective method was not being used in a systematic way. And finally, the notion of self clearly implied the existence

---

[1] The cultural anthropologist Dorothy Lee has observed (1959) that among the Wintu Indians of Northern California there is no word for "self." Grammatical analysis reveals that the Wintus do have a conception of self, but no clear delineation between self and the environment or other persons.

of some activity or entity *internal* to the person. Concepts referring to internal phenomena had little place in early positivism; they were considered empty because they did not refer to anything that was concrete or observable. Concepts referring to stimuli, overt responses, and environmental reinforcement were prime. Concepts that could not be tied directly to the observable world were held to be mysterious if not mythical.

Behaviorism could certainly be attractive. In contrast to the myriad of conflicting opinions about the nature of experience, the behaviorists offered statistical results from highly controlled laboratory experiments. Rather than take the word of a single individual examining his own consciousness in a unique setting, the behaviorists attempted to use multiple subjects, uncontaminated by theoretical bias, in such a way that the experiments could be repeated from one laboratory to the next with the same outcome. Instead of thrashing out a terminology for the subjective world, they concentrated on the manipulation and control of external stimuli and methods for precisely measuring observable behavior.

Conflict developed, however, when what had been a fresh and exciting point of view became dogma. The behaviorist movement at its height turned on its subjectively oriented predecessors with vindictiveness. This proved unfortunate in many ways. First, theoretical insights into the nature of human behavior, even when unsupported by fact, can often lead to useful and innovative research departures. Second, the examination of conscious experience need not stop at the individual level; one can expose large numbers of persons to the same stimulus and utilize standard recording devices. The inspiration for such work must often begin at the level of individual experience. In addition, to concentrate on the control and measurement of stimulus and response, while excluding all consideration of internal process seems naively narrow-minded. To rule out of order notions such as "love," "hate," "thought," "hope," and "self" is to become oblivious to the major concerns of life. The behavioristic quest for experimental control had also taken the path of least resistance and relied primarily on animals for generating data. This, of course, raised severe doubts about the utility of the resulting principles for understanding behavior at the human level.

Thus, in spite of their second-class status and their continuously diminishing numbers, self-psychologists, along with others whose orientation was primarily cognitive or humanistic, persisted in their endeavors. Their tenacity was well rewarded. During the late 1930s and the early 1940s, cracks began to develop in the armor of hard-line positivism. For one, experiments began to show that animals could learn and retain information from the environment without the benefit of reinforcement. Rats could learn a great deal about a maze without ever having been rewarded for finding the way to a goal. In effect, some internal change had been wrought in the organism, and its behavior could not be understood with reference to observables alone. In other experiments, laboratory animals were simply raised in an environment where various designs were displayed in view. Later, without ever having made an external response to these designs or having been rewarded for reacting to them, they were better able to learn distinctions among them than a control group that had not seen the designs. Again, some internal process had been affected, and there was little way to explain it without reference to the murky world of the interior. The role of reinforcement seemed a secondary one, namely, to cause the organism to make active use of information that it had already stored on a cognitive level.

Learning theorists were thus finding that in order to make precise predictions it was necessary to develop concepts encompassing activities or events that were internal to the organism—in other words, that were not readily observable. In order to do this, and at the same time to avoid sacrificing objectivity, psychologists gave a good deal of thought to the relationship between the internal and the external. Over time, the wisest solution to the problem of internal process seemed to be to admit into theory only *certain* concepts relevant to this level—those which were useful in explaining the impact of the stimulus world on the external behavior of the organism. Optimally, this required specification of (1) the way in which variations in stimuli would affect the internal activity or event, and (2) the way in which the internal state would affect behavior. Concepts dealing with the internal were often called *hypothetical constructs* in order to ensure that no one confused such concepts with those for which there were observable referents.

In this way the concept of "hunger drive" could be admitted to the scientific realm. One could say that the number of hours an organism was deprived of food (observable and quantifiable) has a direct effect on the amount of hunger drive. And it could also be hypothesized that the greater the hunger drive the greater the amount of behavioral effort expended in obtaining food. By the same token, the concept of "soul" was not considered admissible. It was unclear not only which environmental events impinged on the soul but, in addition, how different states of the soul would affect behavior.

This loosening of the positivistic strictures also opened the door to a respectable reassessment of the concept of self. It was clear that the positivistic emphasis had had salutory effects. Investigators attempted to be much more systematic. Most preferred to jettison the global term "self" altogether; in this way they could confine their interests to specific sub-aspects or dimensions that would yield to precise definition. Thus, investigators have focussed on "self-esteem," "self-alienation," or "body image" alone. These more clearly delineated enterprises also lent themselves to greater precision in measurement, and thus to greater reliance on empirical fact. Experimentation with reliable samples became a necessity.

As an example of the latter approach, we may utilize the concept of self-esteem (the extent to which the person feels positive about himself) and hypothesize that various levels of self-esteem are reflected in differences in self-report. That is, a person with high-esteem should be more likely to report that "he does not often feel inferior to others." Such self-reports can be standardized and subjected to a variety of methods for establishing validity. We can further predict that the behavior of others affects the level of one's self-esteem; for example, criticism from another should lower self-esteem. Such a prediction can be tested with a large number of subjects and statistical techniques can be applied. We can also predict that differences in self-esteem are systematically related to differences in overt behavior. Here we might speculate that persons high in self-esteem are more likely to set higher standards of performance for themselves. Again, such a prediction can be tested in a replicable way. Such research is a far cry from that which preceded the positivistic period and places the study of self on much more solid footing. More than 2000 empirical studies have accumulated since the 1940s; such research will furnish the factual bases of our later discussions.

ORGANIZATION OF THE VOLUME

This book is organized into four major parts. In Part I we have glimpsed the importance of the concept of self over the centuries, and discussed the study of self as it has progressed through history. In Part II we shall first take a close look at the problem of definition. In doing so, we shall confront a number of issues around which long-standing controversy has centered. We shall then be in a position to develop the rudiments of a contemporary theory of self-conception.

Part III will examine a number of factors that contribute to self-conception—how the person comes to perceive himself as he does. In Part IV we shall turn from a consideration of the ways in which self-conception is shaped by the environment to the part played by the self in shaping behavior. Here we shall be especially concerned with the effects of self-conception on the character of interpersonal relationships. In both Part III and Part IV there will be a strong reliance on empirical research which should serve to add credibility to the various theoretical statements that are developed. The empirical emphasis should increase the reader's appreciation of the power of experimentation as well as his sophistication in contemporary methodology.

It is hoped that this brief account of theory and research on the self will excite the reader to explore more deeply on his own. This invitation to further exploration takes the additional form of an annotated bibliography at the end of the book.

II

Self-Conception:
Critical Issues in Theory

NOW THAT WE HAVE GAINED HISTORICAL PERSPECTIVE, we can begin to ask in earnest about our subject matter, the *self*. We must first come to grips with the complex problem of definition. The term "self" was used in a variety of different ways in Part I; from these multiple meanings, can we possibly extract one upon which we can agree? To lighten our task, we should push past the more romantic, poetic, and metaphoric usages. Essentially we should confine ourselves to a definition that has *scientific utility*. In developing such a definition, we shall deal with issues that have long been troublesome to investigators in the area and undoubtedly the result will reflect our own particular biases. However, if we are successful we should also be aware of the reasons for these biases and hope that if sacrifices are made it will be in the service of gaining scientific foothold.

Any definition contains multiple assumptions. In the present section we shall examine these assumptions in light of recent thinking and research. We noted in Part I that the major research into self during the past decades has often been fragmented into small but manageable segments. We shall use certain of these segments in order to develop a more general, coherent theory. This enlarged theoretical perspective will prove critical, for it will be used as a framework for coordinating the diverse findings presented in the remaining sections of the volume.

TOWARD A DEFINITION OF SELF: ISSUES AND RESOLUTIONS

It would be tedious to read through a list of the many definitions of self found in the extensive literature in the area. For our purposes it is

13

preferable to discuss a number of the central issues that have separated theorists into rival camps. By understanding such confrontation we can attempt to derive solutions that are compatible with contemporary research findings. Viewed in historical perspective, five issues seem most important.

The Self as Fact versus Fiction

For centuries theorists have been prone to speak of the self as if it had substance, just as rocks, trees, flowers, or any other object in the physical world. Theorists such as Berkeley, the philosopher, and Jung, the psychoanalyst, were actually committed to the position of self as a physical entity. Representatives of this position felt, typically, that this entity was made up of experiences of one's personal existence or processes of thinking. For many self-psychologists such a position has a strong attraction—if the self is a physical thing it can be studied scientifically, just as the phenomena of the physical sciences. Scientific respectability can thus be bought for the price of an assumption.

It is clear, however, that the price of this assumption is too dear. It is entirely misleading to think of psychic "phenomena" in the same way as physical objects. Rather, as we saw in Part I, it is much more useful to think in terms of *hypothetical constructs*. A hypothetical concept may be useful in predicting human behavior but does not necessarily refer to real-world objects. Some typical hypothetical constructs include "thought," "perception," "pain," and "hunger." Viewed in this way, the self is much like a "fiction," that is, the notion of self is used *as if* it refers to a fact. Research is continually carried out to assess the utility of using the term in this way—in essence, to establish its truth value. This use of the "fiction" is similar to the notion in astronomy that there is an "orbit" that the earth makes around the sun. An orbit is not a thing, but a concept applied to explain a body which appears to occupy various positions in space at various times. If the concept did not enable us to make numerous predictions, and to verify them, it would most likely be abandoned.

While there is much wisdom in accepting a notion like self on hypothetical grounds, caution must be maintained. There is a strong tendency to reify concepts, to assume that all words must have observable referents. People were at one time fully committed to the "fact" that the sun orbited the earth. If this hypothetical notion had not been accepted as fact, less blood might have been shed in early times. In the same way, if we speak often enough about the "soul" or the "will," it will be relatively easy to be convinced that they actually exist. Both concepts are hypothetical, but our language does not make a distinction between the way we use these words and the way we use those which are tied directly to real-world events. We have concepts referring to oranges, apples, and grapes—directly observable phenomena—but our linguistic habits do not differ when we talk about these as opposed to hypothetical entities. As a result, we tend to believe in the hypothetical as "real."

The Self as Knower versus the Known

A number of theorists have equated self with the process of active experience. For them, the content of experience is of little importance in contrast to the *process* of experiencing or knowing itself. As one early theorist put it, "If consciousness as content exists and content can only exist as content of a subject I, then the experiencing self must exist by the same right as the experienced content" (Calkins, 1912, p. 28). Thus, a process of *active experiencing* is said to exist, and this process is filled with various contents or experiences from moment to moment. Along similar lines, the contemporary psychoanalyst Erik Erikson has argued that the specific contents of experience are not so important in furnishing the person with an identity or a sense of self. Rather it is the capacity of the person to recognize *continuity*—the fact that separate experiences belong to the same being—that is central to self-definition. John Stuart Mill also addressed himself to this process of continuity and in 1865 wrote, "the *inexplicable tie* . . . which connects the present consciousness with the past one of which it reminds me, is as near as I think we can get to a positive conception of self." In effect, the "self" for Mill is equated with the active, experiencing agent. Contents of experience do not figure in the definition.

In contrast, many theorists have been discontent with the position that self should be defined as the experiencer or knower. They argue, for one thing, that all experience is experience *of* something; experience has content, whether it be the book in front of us or the feeling of nausea in the pit of the stomach. The self then, is not the process of experiencing or knowing, but that which is *known*. Second, they argue that if self is defined as the *process* of active experience, the notion of self is suddenly expanded to include so much as to lose all its value. If the study of self is equated with the study of the experiencing agent, then it would be necessary to include under this topic all mental processes—sensing, organizing, remembering, conceptualizing, judging, inductive and deductive reasoning, and so on. The notion of self becomes devoid of precise meaning when used to refer to the entire conglomeration of mental processes.

Is there any way of avoiding the pitfalls contained in each of these opposing positions: the self as the experiencing agent or knower versus the self as what is known? One notable solution was proposed by William James at the turn of the century. James argued that there were not two separate phenomena, the knower and the known, but one. This single phenomenon was the *stream of consciousness,* in which images, emotions, and sensations constantly flowed. The stream of consciousness, however, could be viewed in separate ways. One could choose to study the images or feelings as they were experienced by the person. This was termed the *self as known* or, in shortened form, the object pronoun *me.* Or one could investigate this stream of consciousness by searching for laws or principles governing its operation from moment to moment. For example, why does one thought lead to another? Why do certain memories tend to recur more than others? Mental process can thus be viewed as *self as knower* or, in brief form, the subject pronoun *I.* However, under no circumstances were the I and the Me to be viewed as separate entities. They were to be considered *discriminated aspects* of the same phenomenon.

Certainly James' view is a welcome one. It allows for the study of raw experience without sacrificing consideration of the way in which the experience is ordered or processed. At the same time it is inclusive and avoids fragmentation. But is James' solution sufficient for today? It would seem not. We have already seen that we cannot accept such a notion as "stream of consciousness" as a physical reality. Even if we accept the notion on a hypothetical basis, as it seems desirable to do, how can we study its "discriminated aspects"? First, how can we deal with "experience" or raw sensation on a methodological basis? What are its indicators? Clearly we cannot measure it directly as there is no direct access to another's private experience. The most we can do is to *infer* the nature of a particular experience from various overt behavioral indicators. What overt indicators might one utilize?

First, physiological measures might be employed. Physiology is amenable to precise quantification, and there are certain physiological correlates of what people seem to experience as fear, hostility, and sexual desire, for example. Physiological measures might thus be considered one key to unlocking the door to experience.

Unfortunately, this approach is not yet possible, and many doubt its future as a means of exploring experience. For one thing, there are numerous detectable physiological changes in the body which the person is never capable of identifying. Body temperature, brain waves, and gastric motility, for instance, may all be altered beyond the ken of awareness. In a manner of speaking, they take place unconsciously. Secondly, physiological indicators do not reflect many of the differences in what people say they experience. People are quite capable of distinguishing among resentment, self-hatred, homocidal impulses, and jealousy, and yet the observable physiology is roughly similar for all.

Theorists such as Schachter (1964) have even felt that physiological arousal is gross and undifferentiated. Physiological arousal alone provides us little in the way of information about ourselves. Information from the environment is required for the person to interpret the meaning of the arousal—in other words, to define the exact nature of the experience. The person may not be able to recognize himself as being fearful, for example, unless he finds some justification in the environment for labeling the arousal as fear. From this viewpoint, physiology alone provides little in the way of useful information about self-experience.

The second major possibility for inferring the nature of experience is the person's verbal behavior. People are able to *talk* about their experiences, and their linguistic output is eminently measurable. Why not use verbal data as a basis for making inferences to the experiential level? There is good reason not to follow this course, and it relates to that phenomenon James defined as the "I." One cognitive process of cardinal importance is that of conceptualizing the stimuli registered in experience. From moment to moment the individual is bombarded by stimuli from both the external environment and the internal, or somatic, world. If such inputs are not grouped or categorized in some orderly and systematic way, confusion would reign and adaptive behavior would be rendered impossible. If, from the welter of sense data, we were not able to distinguish among various configurations, between liquids and solids or between fire and ice, life would indeed be short.

At present the single best representation of the way in which the individual conceptualizes the world is given in his verbal habits. His ways of grouping events in the world are indicated most clearly in his language. In terms of James' distinction, verbal behavior is much more closely akin to cognitive process and its products, to the I, than it is to raw experience, or the Me. It provides the best measure of the ways in which the individual organizes sense data, rather than the registering of the sense data themselves.

In essence, then, we have little way of assessing the raw experience of self. But how great a handicap is this? How necessary is it that the experiences themselves be measured? On the one hand, we have a good scientific grip on the inputs to the organism. Scientists have proved quite skillful in developing methods for quantifying the stimulus world impinging on the person from without. If we have access to the verbal behavior, response indicators of how the person categorizes or sorts the stimuli, how necessary is it to have additional access to the "experience" of what he has received? For example, if we know that adding five pounds to a person's normal body weight causes him to categorize himself as "overweight," and subtracting five pounds causes him to label himself "underweight," is it necessary to have additional access to his raw experience of body weight?

We may further ask whether the concept is not more important than the objective experience in influencing behavior. The experience of working at a task has little significance for the individual until he is able to label his activities as "industrious" or "ineffective." The raw stimulus of a red letter on a term paper is of little consequence except as the person categorizes its significance as excellent, mediocre, or failing. A person's concern with his own behavior is heightened dramatically at the point when it is labeled "neurotic" or "queer."

To conclude, the role of sensory experience in the present analysis is a secondary one. At times it will be to our advantage to consider its possible functions but our primary attention will be directed elsewhere. Specifically, we shall center our concern on the way in which people interpret themselves, their actions, or their sensory inputs. The concern, then, is with the *concept* of self rather than with experience.

The Self as Structure versus Process

The third issue of traditional debate need not concern us for long. However, it is important to realize the difference between considering the self a psychological structure, on the one hand, and a process on the other. The term *structure* in this case implies a stable entity (hypothetical) which, by analogy, might function as a part in a machine. We would be taking the structural approach if we spoke of a man's concept of himself as "trial lawyer" being so firmly implanted that it influenced him to be argumentative, even on social occasions. The "concept of self" in this case is treated as if it were a *thing*, having structural properties that give it stability through time.

In contrast, a concentration on *process* would entail discussing principles of operation or forces at play. To continue the above analogy, rather than concentrating on the individual parts of the machine, this approach would focus on the laws underlying its operation. Rather than concentrating on valves, it would center on principles of combustion. In the case of the trial lawyer, we might discuss the process which caused him to conceptualize himself in this way on inappropriate occasions.

For our purposes, there is little reason to belabor this distinction; these approaches need not be seen as mutually exclusive, but rather as complementary ways of approaching the same subject matter. In the preceding section we decided to devote our attention primarily to the *process* of conceptualizing experience and the ways in which this process influences behavior, rather than to the raw experience itself. This approach need not rule out considerations of structure; processes involve the operation of entities. To explain the principles underlying the operation of a machine entails speaking of the ways in which its parts work together. In the same way, a discussion of *concepts* and their characteristics is integral to understanding the process of conceptualizing. Later in this part, for example, we shall see that concepts may differ from one another in a variety of significant ways. In Part III we shall examine actual concepts that various people use to describe themselves. These discussions are highly useful because they freeze the process momentarily and allow an understanding of its constituent parts. In effect, the approaches through process and structure both serve as useful models for discussing the cognition of self.

The Self: One or Many?

When we view the self from the point of view of structure, we are immediately faced with another age-old argument. Is the self better considered a single, or global entity, or is self-conception fragmented, disconnected, and multiple? The way in which we talk about a person's *concept* or *view* of himself suggests that we largely think of the self in the singular. A good deal of research is also premised on this position. For example, in Part IV when we discuss self-esteem, we shall look at a number of research studies that have attempted to measure self-esteem and to use these measures for predicting behavior. The underlying assumption is that the person has some single, basic concept of himself as good or bad, superior or inferior, and that this concept will have a marked impact on his social conduct. If a person feels he is basically superior, it might be predicted that he would tend to treat others as his inferiors.

Yet there are strong arguments against this position of singular conceptualization of self. For one, if a person is asked to describe himself, he will typically use a large number of different concepts that have little or no relationship to each other. Former President Lyndon Johnson once described himself as "a free man, an American, a United States Senator, a Democrat, a liberal, a conservative, a Texan, a taxpayer, a rancher, and not as young as I used to be nor as old as I expect to be." Not only are many of these characteristics unrelated, but some even contradict each other—such as "liberal" and "conservative," "free man" and "taxpayer." It also seems clear that not all these various concepts are equally relevant at all times and that at certain moments the concept of self as "Senator" was much more important to Johnson than the concept of being "older than before." As we shall see, such tendencies in describing self are very common.

In summary, the assumption of a single, or global, concept of self seems misleading. Rather than speaking of *the* self or self-concept, it is much more fruitful to speak of multiple conceptions.

Self-Consistency versus Inconsistency

While the structural approach leads us into the problem of one versus many, an emphasis on process has its own parallel problems. The most cogent debate concerns the relationship among the various concepts a person has of himself. More specifically, given that the person has multiple concepts of self, do these multiple views remain fragmented and inconsistent or do they tend over time toward harmony and compatibility?

This question has not always been stated in such dispassionate terms. For many centuries Western man has railed against inconsistency, damning the individual who displays incompatibilities. Biblical scriptures condemn the man who is "double-minded" or who "serves two masters." Shakespeare's characters ask for behavior consistent with the "true" self; damaging labels such as forked tongue, traitor, liar, duplicitous, are given to those who have acted inconsistently. To some extent, such hostility results from the fact that the inconsistent person has broken a trust, and as a result someone has been vitally harmed. However, even when trust and harm are not at stake, the value judgment seems to persist. Even William James, in his more impulsive moments, argued that consistency was to be praised and that the inconsistent were "sick souls."

Some have argued that to demand thoroughgoing consistency is to surround the person with walls against spontaneity and true knowledge about self. However, our concern here is not to draw value judgments or argue about "shoulds." Rather, the question is what psychological model best accounts for behavior. To what extent can we characterize a person's multiple concepts of self as internally incompatible and to what extent do they tend toward consistency?

There is good evidence that the more typical state is one in which incompatibility reigns. First, there are self-reports such as that of President Johnson in which inconsistency is highly apparent. There are also studies such as the classic by Hartshorne and May (1928) which indicate that a person's so called "character traits" are not highly pervasive but specific to certain specific circumstances. Because a person is deceitful or dishonest in one situation is little reason to suspect that he will tend to be that way in others. Further, there is research on the presentation of self, to be described in Part IV, that demonstrates marked discrepancies between the way a person views himself from one situation to another.

Such evidence is also congruent with notions of concept learning. The learning approach holds that a person can acquire varying conceptions of self in different situations. He can learn a certain way of conceptualizing himself from his father and possibly an opposite way from his younger brothers. In the former case he may come to see himself as "submissive" and in the latter, "dominant." When these situations recur and, more specifically, when the people within them reappear, they act as stimuli to elicit the particular conceptions learned in the past. A father may cause his son to remember himself as "submissive" and brothers may elicit the conception that he is "dominant."

And yet, we cannot close the case so simply in the light of the voluminous literature on dissonance reduction. Dissonance theory (Festinger, 1957; Brehm & Cohen, 1962) essentially states that inconsistent cognitions or thoughts are intolerable for human beings. Whenever one experiences inconsistency among his thoughts, he will go to great lengths to eliminate the discrepancies. According to the theory, if faced with information that he is both dominant and submissive, intelligent and stupid, or honest and dishonest, one will feel discomfort. Further, he will set about ridding himself of the inconsistencies in one of a variety of ways. Although not all of the evidence is unequivocal, over 500 experimental investigations in this area lead to the conclusion that such a tendency indeed exists. Western culture simply does not seem prone to accepting both a proposition and its antithesis simultaneously.

How can we resolve these antagonistic viewpoints? What should we conclude about the tendency to reduce inconsistency in self-conception? Clearly qualification is needed and such qualification can be broken down into three parts. In the first instance, a basic tenet in dissonance theory is that the intolerable state of dissonance only exists when the person is *cognizant* of the relationship between two cognitions. Thus, if a man considers himself a "tough realist" at the office and a "gentle sentimentalist" at home, he may experience little dissonance because of the separate conditions under which they are salient. However, if both conceptions were elicited simultaneously, such as when the children are taken to the office, dissonance might result. In this case, the person would be directly confronted with the inconsistency.

A second factor affecting tolerance for self-inconsistency is related to the *functional value* of the concepts involved. If someone receives a great deal of gratification from thinking of himself in one way and equally great rewards from considering himself the antithesis, considerable dissonance might be expected. If the concepts of self are of little consequence to the person, he might well be indifferent to their illogicality. Thus, for example, a young man might take great pride in considering himself a "cool swinger" and receive much reinforcement from his male friends for behaving as such. On the other hand, his special girl might reward him greatly for thinking of himself as "straight and devoted." Coming to grips with these inconsistencies might be very difficult for the individual. If, on the other hand, the "cool swinger" is also faced with the cognition of himself as "an occasional babysitter for his younger brother," he might experience dissonance, but of a less tense variety. Watching over his younger brother would probably have little functional value for him, being a conception of self that yields little reward or punishment from the environment.

Turning now to a third qualification, we may assume that there is no genetic basis for the tendency to reduce dissonance. The person essentially *learns* to dislike inconsistency in the same way that he learns how to reason inductively and deductively. More importantly, just as training in the application of logical processes differs from person to person, so may there be differences among persons in their training in dissonance reduction. Some persons may be little concerned with the inconsistencies they discover in themselves; others may set out on long courses of self-correction or improvement when they locate contradictory selves. Such individual differences will be discussed further later.

We may conclude, then, that inconsistency in concepts of self may be perfectly natural and widespread. At the same time there may be a generalized tendency to reduce inconsistency. The extent of this tendency will largely depend on the individual's awareness of the inconsistency, the functional value of the concepts at stake, and the amount of training he has had in avoiding inconsistency.

COMPONENTS OF A DEFINITION

In the search for a viable definition of self, we have had to face up to issues that have long provoked argument in the field. Perhaps we can crystallize the biases we have developed thus far into a definition. The notion of self can be defined first as process and then as structure. On the former level we shall be concerned with *that process by which the person conceptualizes (or categorizes) his behavior—both his external conduct and his internal states.* On a structural level, our concern is with *the system of concepts available to the person in attempting to define himself.*

SELF-CONCEPTION: A SOCIO-COGNITIVE APPROACH

Now that we have derived a definition of self, we are equipped to elaborate a more complete theory. Later, in Parts III and IV, we shall be able to examine evidence stemming from these theoretical statements in more detail.

Why a Process of Conceptualization?

The life of the human being is dominated by concepts. His manner of sorting and classifying events is central in determining the course of his activities. His treatment of certain objects or stimuli as equivalent, but as different from certain others, is vital to his continued existence. In the Darwinian sense, the ability to conceptualize has *survival value.* To be more specific, concepts are valuable tools in problem solving. If the environment appears to the child initially as random flux, his ability to recognize and classify events in it will be crucial to his gaining control. Classification allows him to use the environment to achieve rewards instead of being its victim. The child who quickly recognizes that each time he emits a vocal sound of high pitch and volume he is nurtured is the child who is able to secure loving care from his mother whenever he needs it.

The conceptual process also contributes to the survival of the species in several other ways. If objects or events can be recognized as falling into categories, then learning can be generalized from one situation to another; knowledge can be cumulative. If a child finds that liquid substances which emit vapor are painful to touch, his ability to conceptualize such stimuli and responses will allow him to avoid many painful experiences in the future. The ability to classify, then, allows the person to accumulate knowledge and to avoid constant and often painful relearning.

Human communication is also greatly facilitated by the capacity to form concepts. When verbal behavior becomes associated with concepts (for example, the *word* fish becomes associated with the mental *concept* of fish) people become capable of communicating vast amounts of knowledge rapidly and efficiently. Suppose that in a primitive locale, all fish having black scales, large fins, and small eyes at a certain season of the year were poisonous, but that when these characteristics were altered, the fish became edible. This would be valuable information for the local inhabitants to pass on. Without concepts for grouping these various attributes, the communication of the message would be impossible. When the concepts are available and words attached to them, the community quickly becomes more adaptive.

Finally, it can be conjectured that people develop concepts in order to reduce or avoid anxiety. It has been clear so far that the individual repeatedly learns that classification is necessary if he is going to survive—to avoid pain and receive pleasure. As a result of this indelible lesson, he should come to avoid situations in which he is unable to classify stimuli. By implication, such situations constitute a threat to survival—the inability to classify signifies to the individual that control of the stimulus or adaptive responses to it are less within his grasp, and that pain or punishment might ensue at any moment. In essence, there may be a strong learned need for persons to conceptualize phenomena; when they are unable to do so they become anxious or fearful. Perhaps events that were incomprehensible to early man, events for which there were no available categories, necessitated developing the concept of God.

Why Concepts of Self?

Thus far we have seen that the conceptual process serves a variety of important functions for the individual. But of what functional value would a series of self-concepts be? In what ways does self-conception aid the individual? First, in problems of social interaction the individual is aided through developing concepts of self. If, for example, a person finds that others are constantly shunning him, he may ask what there is about himself that causes this reaction. Certain observations of his own behavior might lead him to the conclusion that he is "overbearing" and "egotistical." In the same way a concept of one's physical capabilities would be useful before tangling with the school bully or an assessment of one's value to others could be helpful before running the risk of confessing a wicked deed.

Second, self-conception is valuable in allowing the individual to form generalizations about himself that persist over time. Knowledge about self is thus allowed to accumulate, and the individual need not engage in constant relearning. If the person learns that he is easily provoked to anger when he drinks large quantities of alcohol, he may use this self-knowledge to avoid over-indulgence on future occasions. If he believes that he performs better when he has an audience, he may take special care to ensure that others are present when his performance is important.

The efficacy of human communication is also greatly increased through the availability of self-concepts. To inform a person that you are "strong-willed, energetic, cheerful, and curious" is to provide in an instant information about yourself that might otherwise require a very long time to obtain. The computerized dating and mating systems that have recently flourished in the United States depend almost entirely on the individual's capacity to summarize his observations of himself in brief, conceptual form. Placement in almost any formal organization, whether religious or military, social service or business, depends on this same capacity. An individual who does not possess a sizable number of labels for himself has a truly difficult time in contemporary society.

A learned need to categorize may in fact influence the person to develop a set of concepts of self. We spoke in Part I about the question "who am I" that seems so important to so many. Perhaps the question would be much less important if the person did not experience some degree of anxiety whenever he lacked a set of ready definitions. Investigators have often singled out adolescence as the time in which the problem of identity is most acute (see Erikson, 1959). Our theory of the need to conceptualize may be helpful in understanding why this is so. Adolescence is typically a time in which old labels are no longer applicable. One's earlier ways of defining himself in relation to his body, his parents, and the opposite sex all become inappropriate during adolescence. Because of the learned need to conceptualize and the accompanying fear at no longer having applicable labels, adolescence may well be a time in which an "identity crisis" occurs.

The Development of Concepts

Now that we have seen how crucial the conceptual process is, and examined several functions of self-conception, we can turn to a second important issue: how are concepts developed? How does the person come to possess the particular set of concepts at his disposal?

To answer this question it is necessary to distinguish among three separate aspects of the process, two of them already familiar to us. We must first deal with the process of *sensation,* the individual's experience of raw sense data. On this level it is important to realize that the person is furnished with physiological equipment that renders him sensitive to extremely fine differences between stimuli. In color perception alone one is capable of discriminating some seven and a half million separate colors.

The second aspect is the *cognitive* one, in which the person begins to group certain of these stimuli together. The color spectrum, with millions of discriminable colors, is represented by only a dozen or so concepts.

On the cognitive level it must first be noted that the person is capable of grouping the same stimuli in a multitude of ways. If given an assortment of diverse objects, one would have little difficulty in sorting them on the basis of several different criteria such as color, size, and so on. Second, it is clear that such groupings can take place on a purely cognitive basis. That is, reward or punishment from without is not necessary for classification or grouping to take place on a cognitive level. The physiological reaction may differ so dramatically from stimulus to stimulus that concepts may be derived on a purely sensory basis. Sensory distinctions can be made, for instance, between black and white, sharp and blunt, sweet and sour. On the level of self, the differences between standing and sitting, running and walking, or fear and happiness might also be categorized or differentiated without the aid of learning.

A discussion of sensation and cognition alone, however, is entirely inadequate. People utilize only a small proportion of the concepts available to them. When confronted with a myriad of separate color configurations, we lump them all under the single concept, "sunset." And what irritation we feel when someone is confronted with many varieties of pleasure and refers to them all as "nice." How can we account for the fact that we use so few of the concepts potentially available to us? Moreover, certain groupings of stimuli and not others are used. If the same behavior can be labeled both "dignified" and "snobbish," what causes the person to choose one label rather than the other? In the case of color, it has been found that not all cultures use the same division of the spectrum. Where some cultures use two concepts, such as blue and green, others may include all hues within this range in a single category (see Brown's discussion, 1958). Such phenomena cannot be accounted for by simple differences in physiological reaction.

In order to deal with these facts we must turn to a third aspect of the conceptual process, that which is *reinforcement dependent*. We have already seen that the individual is capable of registering sensations and grouping them on the basis of intrinsic differences in physiological reaction. Yet, we have also seen in our discussion of the functional value of concepts that concept usage can be dependent on reinforcement from the environment. Reinforcement is the reason we reduce the spectrum of potential concepts to a manageable few and the reason we select one concept rather than another in any particular instance. Children are rewarded from a very early age for responding to the many changing hues and patterns at the close of the day with the single concept, "sunset." And if people respond to wide variety of stimuli with the single concept, "nice," it is partially the fault of their nice friends. The selection of one concept over another is also highly dependent on reinforcement. An individual may be warmly received for referring to his friend's behavior as "dignified," but the use of "snobbish" might result in the loss of his friend. Similarly, there is considerable reward in our culture for using both the concepts "blue" and "green." If one did not make just this distinction he might even be rejected from the military draft. In other cultures, to make this distinction might yield disapproval for excessive quibbling about color differences.

Reward and punishment do not simply reduce the concept range and influence which concepts are used. Gratification and avoidance of pain also encourage the person to develop new classifications or concepts. At times it is to our advantage to classify stimuli on the basis of extremely subtle differences in sense data, differences to which we might not otherwise attend. As the early linguist Benjamin Lee Whorf pointed out, Eskimos distinguish among eight different types of snows, while persons in more temperate zones make few if any such distinctions. It is not that the more southerly neighbor is unable to make the same distinctions; it is rather that there is little functional value for him to discern such subtle differences among stimuli.

Reward and punishment may also cause the person to develop novel groupings that have little connection with differences in sensation. The fact that we include such diverse physical objects as rifles, tanks, and planes under the single concept of "weapons" attests to this. Abstract concepts such as "purity," "power," or "soul" have even more remote connections with the world of sense data. But because the use of such concepts is rewarded in contemporary society, they become part of our standard way of understanding our environment and ourselves.

The Relevance of Language

In order to communicate about concepts it has been necessary to use their verbal representatives. In order to express the concepts of "blue" and "green" we have had to use the associated words. However, we must always bear in mind the distinction between the mental world of concepts and the external domain of language. To be sure, there is a close relationship between the two—almost all words used in human communication are represented on the mental or concept level, although words in foreign languages often do not have mental equivalents for us. Essentially, however, people use words to express concepts and most concepts that people use with great frequency eventually come to be represented in their vocabulary. In the initial stages of the LSD vogue, participants often complained that there were no words adequate to communicate their experiences. Years later, dozens of books were filled with verbal descriptions. A language had been develop so that concepts could be communicated.

At the same time, the verbal world has a powerful impact on the concept world. From the time the child learns to speak, the way in which he conceptualizes the world is also beng affected. Our language reflects the agreements of the culture as to how the stimulus world should be differentiated and rendered accountable. The common ways of distinguishing between "good" and "bad," among social classes within culture, among activities or behaviors, are all represented in the language. To learn the language is to adopt the concept system inherent in it. When the child is reinforced positively for using the word "hot" in the presence of certain stimulus configurations and negatively for using the term in others, he is learning that there is a class of stimuli to which the term applies.

This reasoning is especially pertinent to understanding self-conception. In the case of self, stimulus ambiguity abounds. The physical differences between one behavior or internal bodily activity and another are often difficult to discern and do not often lend themselves to intrinsic categorization; behavioral activity moves at a rapid pace and provides a myriad of stimuli. In watching an athlete run a hundred-yard dash it is not an overstatement to say that we are exposed to more discriminably different stimuli than the 7½ million furnished by the color spectrum. In observing his own behavior the individual is bombarded with information from moment to moment.

The individual's manner of conceptualizing behavior—and most pertinently his own—is vitally dependent on the linguistic system within his culture. A person may sit in hundreds of discriminably different postures, move his arms in varying paths, move his mouth at various odd intervals, utter various sounds, look in various directions, all within a period of an hour, and we all agree to label this welter of sense data "eating." Why do we not have several categories to discriminate various stages of this behavior; why not a hundred categories; why not a thousand? We use the simple label primarily because the language has made it functional for us to do so. In the same way we have highly biased ways of determining what behavior we label "studying," what constitutes "loafing," and what is, or is not, "sexual" behavior. And we arbitrarily divide internal states into categories such as "happiness," "depression," and "anger" although our internal existence could be sorted in far different ways.

This argument goes further than saying that language influences which behaviors or internal events are sorted into which conceptual bins;

in fact, the very bins themselves are furnished by the language. We might consider, for example, many of the concepts so widespread in middle-class America, if not in all Western society. We are highly prone to sort out our own behavior on the basis of whether or not it is "productive," "honest," "helpful to others," and "useful." And we all have a strong propensity to ask ourselves whether our actions are "good" or "bad." Socialization not only teaches us what behaviors fall into each of these categories, but also influences the fact that we use such categories in the first place. It is quite possible to conceive of a culture in which such concepts are not applied at all; anthropological studies bring such cultures into clear focus. However, the process of learning a language engenders a strong commitment to conceptual habits, and it is doubtful that many of us would find such cultures very satisfying places in which to live.

The present discussion should not be concluded without attention to individual differences. The socialization process is seldom uniform, and individuals are infrequently exposed to precisely the same learning experiences as they grow and develop. Therefore, we can assume that (1) not all individuals will agree as to which behaviors fall into which categories, and (2) various concepts may differ in their importance for different individuals. With respect to self-conception, two persons may behave in the "same way," but the way they categorize this behavior may differ greatly. Such differences are especially important in terms of the categories "good" and "bad," which we will find to play a central role in emotional life. For anyone concerned with furthering human happiness, it is striking to observe two individuals engaging in precisely the same activity, one coming away with a sense of glowing fulfillment and the other feeling depressed and remorseful.

The fact that certain concepts may be more important or relevant for one individual than for another has broad implications. Child-rearing practices may differ from family to family in terms of the functional value of certain conceptual habits. Thus, one family may constantly push its children to evaluate themselves in terms of "achievement" standards; another may constantly ask the children how "happy" they feel. Children in the former case may continue to evaluate and define themselves according to achievement criteria long after leaving the family, while the latter group may seldom question their achievements but may base crucial decisions on the presence or absence of happiness.

We shall return to the problem of the development of self-conception in Part III. There we shall examine at close range a series of studies that demonstrate and expand on many of the influences that we have discussed.

DIMENSIONS OF THE CONCEPTUAL WORLD

Thus far we have defined self-conception, we have seen why the conceptual process is so important, and we have discussed how concepts are developed in the context of both language and culture. It remains finally to focus more sharply on the nature of concepts—more specifically, we must ask about ways in which concepts differ from one another. We have already seen two important ways in which concepts may be compared. For one, we have pointed to differences in the *content* of various concepts; for example, our concept of "green" simply refers to a different set of stimuli than our concept of "blue." We have also discussed how concepts may differ from one another in *functional value*; some concepts are reinforced more than others. But we must now include additional dimensions of self-conception which will further enable us to understand an individual's behavior.

Differentiation

When presented with a large array of stimuli, persons may differ markedly with respect to the number of subgroups which they distinguish. As in the case of the color spectrum, some persons may differentiate only six or seven colors, lumping all shades into these groupings. Artists or dress designers, however, may use from 30 to 50 different concepts to account for the same array. Lipstick manufacturers even have a score of categories to account for various shades of red. Such conceptual systems are highly differentiated with respect to color.

It also follows from our earlier discussion of functional value that the amount of differentiation will depend largely on the rewards or punishments received. A football coach is able to describe a given play in much more detail than a cheerleader, and an astronomer is able to discriminate among galaxies far better than the man on the street. Their professional lives depend on their doing so. Language learning undoubtedly has a great deal to do with the amount of differentiation that occurs. Learning how to apply words to various stimuli is learning ways of grouping these stimuli. In effect, the person with the larger vocabulary has more potential for rapid and precise grouping of various phenomena.

Differentiation may also be an important factor in self-conception. A person who considers himself a "pacifist," for instance, will tend to see his behavior as *either* "aggressive" *or* "pacifistic" and will try to ensure that he will never have to apply the former label to himself. Other people might use three concepts rather than two in sorting this aspect of their behavior. They may agree as to what is pacifistic but distinguish, at the same time, various types of aggressive behavior. They do not wish to see themselves as exploitatively aggressive but find that aggression in the service of self-defense quite another matter. The long-standing and sometimes bloody confrontation between pacifists and nonpacifists can be viewed partially as a disagreement over essential ways of differentiating the world.

The extent to which one's view of self is differentiated may have wide consequences. To take only one example, a lack of differentiation may cause one to be more easily distressed by failure or criticism. Consider for a moment the woman whose major conception of herself is "housewife." Within this broad category fall a number of diverse behaviors such as cooking, cleaning, taking care of baby, shopping, paying bills, and so on. Little distinction is made among these activities; they all fall within the undifferentiated concept of "housewife." When such a woman is criticized for any one of these activities, the results may be devastating. Each behavior is but an example from a larger category, and pain derived from any exemplar is pain for the entire category. For the woman who maintains clear conceptual distinctions of herself as "cook" as opposed to "mother" or "financial expert," the effects in one area should be far less pronounced. Criticism for her cooking would be taken as condemnation not of a major way of viewing herself, but of only one of a large number of self-aspects. Differentiation, then, insulates against the disturbing effects of social punishment.[1]

Salience

Common observation tells us that not all one's ways of defining the world are relevant to him at any one time. Man is simply not capable of mentally juggling his entire repertoire of concepts at any one instant. Further, he may not even apply the same concepts to a given object from one instant to the next. A particular place may be at one time a "forest," at another a "picnic spot," a "hunting ground," or a "trysting place." The same actions may be defined as "dangerous," "foolish," "heroic," or "vain," depending on time and circumstance. In order to account for the differential use of concepts from moment to moment, we can apply the term *salience*. A concept may vary in its salience to the individual at any given moment, and its salience may depend on a variety of factors.

Three prominent factors may be singled out as affecting concept

---

[1] The relationship between differentiation and mental health has been discussed at length by George Kelly (1955).

salience. First, it is quite clear that the *amount of learning* or training with a given concept is an essential determinant. If a concept has been continuously used with a high degree of success, if the intrinsic organization of events in the world has continuously suggested it, or if one has been continuously exposed to others who use it, the concept should be highly salient. We are quite accustomed, for instance, to classify various types of automobiles according to manufacturer. We see Fords, Buicks, Porsches, and so on. However, there are many other ways in which automobiles can be classified, such as seating capacity, size of wheel base, color of dashboard, and so on. We use the more familiar form of classification simply because we have had much more training with it.

Similarly, a person may learn a variety of ways of viewing himself. However, certain of these conceptions are learned more thoroughly than others. An individual's concept of himself as male or female is typically learned at a very early age, and its usage receives continuous reinforcement—such a concept has a high degree of salience. One may be highly sensitive to any suggestion that he is not acting according to his assigned sex-role. Thirty years ago most Caucasian Americans had little concept of themselves as "white," with all its connotations of a specific culture that differed from others in the same country. In the present day, they are frequently, and often painfully, made aware of this particular aspect of self.

Secondly, the salience of any concept will depend on the *stimulus situation* at a given moment. This proposition also stems from what has been said about the learning of concepts. Learning takes place within specified situations; thereafter, these situations serve as stimuli for the cognitive and behavioral responses learned therein. The ways in which the world is conceptualized inside as opposed to outside the classroom may differ markedly—much to a professor's dismay. A student may spend the better part of a year in being reinforced within class to make distinctions between the schizophrenic, the manic-depressive, and the psychopathic deviate. Within the classroom the concepts eventually become normative. It is painful, then, to hear the same student later tell his friends about his "uncle who is nuts."

Such theorizing is very important to our understanding of self-conception. Parents may continuously reinforce their child for viewing himself as "dependent" and "compliant" even long after childhood. Friends, on the other hand, may treat him with great respect, causing him to view himself as "independent" or "aggressively single-minded." The essential point here is that the subsequent presence of parents should cause the former concept of self to become salient, while the stimulus of friends should be sufficient to bring a much different view of self to mind. In short, one's concept of who he is depends partly on what he has previously learned about himself in the type of situation at hand. In this sense one's identity is situationally dependent.

The third determinant of salience is *motivation*. The primary way in which needs may serve to influence salience is related to the value of concepts for the person, as we discussed earlier. We have seen how concepts are instrumental to the person in helping him to fulfill his needs. If thirsty, for example, a person must locate a substance that falls within the concept of "thirst quenching"; using the concept aids in gratifying the need. The presence of the need, then, should increase the salience of the concept relevant to fulfilling the need.

Here, too, we see important implications for understanding self-conception and its effect on social relationships. Adolescent courtship can have a strong impact on self-conception, laying the foundations of the person's view of himself in relationships with members of the opposite sex through the rest of his life. Some males learn that in order to gain female affection they must define themselves as "strong," "physically attractive," and "fun loving." If putting these concepts of self to use brings success, they should tend to have a high degree of salience during later courtship. Problems do develop, however, when salient concepts no longer have functional value. Success in courtship, for example, may have little to do with success in a marriage relationship. Congratulating oneself on physical appearance and prowess may have disastrous consequences in dealing with a wife whose primary concern has become the creditors at the door. The wife may be unhappy because her husband's behavior seems inappropriate to the situation, and the husband may feel angry because his wife is not providing validation for his concept of himself. She may be seen as somehow turning her back on all the "important" things.

Consistency

Much has been said concerning the issue of unity versus inconsistency in self-conception. There is ample opportunity for inconsistency to develop in the way the person views himself, and at the same time there seems to be a widespread need for persons to rid themselves of such inconsistency. The extent to which this need operates was shown to be dependent on a number of factors, including cognizance of the inconsistency, the functional value of the concepts in question, and the amount of training in inconsistency reduction. One important way of characterizing any given concept of self, therefore, is with respect to how consistent it is with other views the person has of himself. If a person views himself simultaneously as "religious," "strong-principled," "honest," and "a thief," it might be said that the latter concept is weighted most strongly in the direction of inconsistency. Its relationship to the other concepts is more inconsistent than the relationship between any other concept and the remainder.

The degree of consistency attached to any concept may have important consequences for the individual. For one thing, he should be more willing to part with a way of viewing himself that conflicts with many other conceptions of self. The person receiving gratification from being a "banker," a "family man," and a "pillar of the community" might well suppress that part of himself which seems "uninhibited." For much the same reason, students often find it difficult to adjust to the world they enter after college. Those concepts of self found most gratifying during the four years of relative freedom are often incompatible with the reward structure encountered afterwards. This reward structure is usually powerful enough, however, to cause the person to integrate what first seems "alien" into his system of self-conception. As the years proceed, the alien becomes the dominant and many of the most prized aspects of identity in the early years become suppressed as inconsistent. The "impulsive," "romantic," and "independently minded" aspects come to be replaced with concepts such as "banker," "family man," and "pillar of the community."

Self-Evaluation

While it is the last of the dimensions of self to be discussed in this part, *self-evaluation* is hardly the least important. In fact, if we were to judge by the amount of attention that investigators have devoted to the topic, self-evaluation could easily be considered preeminent in its importance. As we shall see in Part IV, the person's evaluation or esteem of himself plays a key role in determining his behavior. A number of prominent theorists in the field of psychiatry have also maintained that self-evaluation is of critical importance in understanding mental illness.

Our discussion of self-conception has thus far been confined to the level of thinking and reasoning. We have seen the similarities between the individual's comprehension of the world at large and his understanding of himself. These more intellective aspects of self-conception can be contrasted with the domain of *emotions*. In dealing with self-evaluation we are essentially adding an emotional component to the network of concepts. Why is this necessary?

First, for any way of conceptualizing the environment there may be an emotional association. This emotional association, or connotation, may be arranged roughly along a dimension of pain–pleasure. Certain concepts carry with them intensely pleasureful associations, others less pleasureful, still others a mixture of pain and pleasure, and some may evoke feelings of great pain. In other words, we could say that concepts have evaluative *loadings* or *weights*. Concepts may vary in the degree to which they are positively or negatively weighted. Typically, the concept of "peace" is weighted in the positive direction while the concept of "war" is negatively weighted. A person may experience pleasure when thinking of himself as an "athlete," but chagrin at his conception of self as "immature."

It is also clear that evaluative connotations are relative; certain people may have very positive feelings about war and others may dislike themselves as athletes. The implication, then, is that the evaluative weighting of a concept is *learned*. In addition, self-evaluation may develop and shift over time as the individual encounters varying learning experiences. Thus, not only does an individual learn to value or devalue himself as "athlete," but the amount of positive feeling the concept provides may fluctuate as various events impinge on him.

But how are these evaluative loadings learned? How can we characterize such processes? The evaluations attached to concepts are largely by-products of the pleasure or displeasure the person experiences as a result of his behavior. A person's behavior may bring him various degrees of satisfaction or dissatisfaction without its being conceptualized in any way. The person may experience pleasure from eating or pain when pricked by a sharp instrument, and neither of these emotional reactions depends on the availability of concepts. However, as we have seen, concepts are developed that apply to such events as eating or being pricked. Indeed, to the extent that an individual receives pleasure or pain from an object or an activity, he will attempt to conceptualize it. Concepts aid in deriving pleasure and avoiding pain. The major point is that because of the *simultaneous occurrence* of an event that yields pleasure and the conceptualization of the event, pleasure becomes associated with the concept. Because eating produces a positive emotional reaction and the concept of "eating" is either developing or salient at the time, the concept becomes associated with the emotion. As time goes on, the concept of eating should be positively weighted for the individual.

We may apply the reasoning thus far to our example of the athlete. The concept of self as "athlete" might be highly salient for the individual as he participates in track events or plays shortstop for the school team. If such behavior brings him pleasure or a sense of satisfaction, the concept of himself participating in these activities should become positively weighted through association. The person might thereafter enjoy thinking of himself as an athlete. However, this enjoyment may be subject to fluctuation. A day of lost races in track or multiple errors as shortstop might temporarily weight the concept negatively. Losing one's berth on the team might alter his feeling of self as "athlete" for a very long time.

Although this particular learning process is important, it can hardly account for the huge repertoire of evaluatively loaded concepts harbored by each individual. We have emotional associations for virtually any activity, regardless of our experience with it. We don't generally like "graft" or "extortion," for instance, though few of us have had any direct encounter with such activities. How then do such concepts become emotionally tinged? The most apparent answer to this question is that we learn through social intercourse and primarily through the vehicle of language. We are exposed daily to a myriad of learning experiences in which concepts are associated with pleasure or pain on the verbal level. Thus, we hear that a certain restaurant is "excellent," a particular novel is "not worth reading," or that a given acquaintance is "very bright." As a result we come away with some increment in feeling, either positive or negative, about the object or person in question. Whenever the concept of the restaurant, book, or person is salient, whenever we *think* of them, the emotional connotation is also likely to be present. And these same connotations may have important effects on our behavior. Where we eat, what we read, and who we associate with are all likely to be affected.

This process is equally applicable to thinking about oneself. There are numerous concepts that may be used in describing persons. We may speak of individuals as fat or lean, black or white, "up-tight" or "groovy," and so on. Largely through verbal interaction such concepts become laden with affect. Our knowledge that people strive in multiple ways to shed pounds is sufficient to invest the concept "fat" with negative overtones. The evaluative attachment to "black person" is currently undergoing a profound revolution in the United States. Formerly the concept often had very negative associations, but a shift in concept usage is evident—on the lips of national figures and in the pages of "black power" newspapers alike. By contrast, emotional investment in the colloquial concepts of "up-tight" and "groovy" is limited to a small minority. Entering this minority requires a rapid learning of the labels, how to apply them, and what their evaluative significance is. Maintaining oneself in this minority may also require a sensitivity to when the terms should be dropped from usage.

But learning the evaluative significance of concepts from the surrounding culture is only a part of the process. One also comes to apply such concepts to himself. He may observe that his own behavior or demeanor falls within a given category, or others may inform him that he is a certain kind of person. When such concepts are applied to self they will carry with them evaluative weight, and it is this weight that forms an integral part of the person's self-esteem. For many, being "fat" is an infinitely depressing state, even though the value of weight is arbitrarily assigned by the immediately surrounding culture. Scientists concerned with racial problems have long noted what they feel to be a debilitating lack of self-esteem among Negroes in the United States. It seems clear that this deficit is in part due to the negative associations of "black" as they have been handed on from one generation to the next. And to be able to define oneself as "groovy," with all its positive overtones, may be a major way of defending oneself against the more critical terms applied to one's behavior by society at large.

In the remainder of this volume we shall often adopt the common term *self-esteem* when speaking of the evaluative component of self-conception. Unfortunately, researchers have tended to think solely in terms of global or fixed levels of self-esteem; that is, they have tended to view people as if some felt they were "inferior" and others felt "superior" (or somewhere in between). Such feelings are assumed to be developed early in life and to be retained from then on. It is clear from earlier discussion that such a view is short-sighted and that people harbor many different conceptions of self—each of which may be weighted differently and may change over time and within situations, depending on a variety of factors. Self-esteem is thus neither global nor fixed.

This argument also has implications for the measurement of self-esteem. Many investigators have assessed self-esteem by having persons rate themselves on a variety of items (for example, "I feel confident in my relations with others"). On the basis of such ratings, global self-esteem levels are imputed, and persons with high self-esteem are then compared to those with low esteem on some behavior or another (conformity, achievement, and so forth). However, gross errors may be committed in assessing self-esteem in this way. A person's self-esteem score may depend entirely on the content of the items the investigator includes in the test. A person whose score is low for items dealing with confidence in social relations might score very high in confidence about his occupational abilities. Feelings of esteem in social as well as occupational areas can also vary over time. Success can inflate esteem at one moment, and failure reduce it at another. In order to avoid such pitfalls, some researchers have altered a particular aspect of the experimental situation, for example, causing subjects to fail at a given task. Hypotheses about the effects of self-esteem on behavior have then been tested with these experimentally created groups.

However, it also is clear that self-rating methods can yield interesting and reasonable findings and are more applicable to certain problems (such as the relationship of self-esteem to psychiatric problems) than the experimental approach. Therefore, if the range of items is broad enough, self-rating may correspond roughly to some of the commonly reinforced evaluations of the person's more salient self-conceptions.

SUMMARY

In this part, we have deemed the question "What is self?" inappropriate because the way in which it is formulated does not lead to conclusions that are scientifically useful. Rather, we have first hypothesized a process by which the individual defines or categorizes his own activities, both internal and external. The resultant *concepts* of self are multiple and often inconsistent. Concepts, particularly self-concepts, play a crucial role in orienting the individual to the world around him and in enabling him to increase his rewards and avoid punishment.

In order to understand the development of concepts it was necessary to distinguish among the *experiential, cognitive,* and *reinforcement dependent* aspects of the process. While the first two aspects allowed speculation about certain intrinsic tendencies toward categorization, the third was viewed as essential in the individual's choice of concepts and his development of fresh modes of understanding. The potent effects of language training in shaping the individual's system of self-conception were also discussed.

Attention was then turned to various dimensions of self-conception. Concepts were seen to differ from one another in their *content* (or referents), in their *functional value* to the individual, and in other ways. Concept *differentiation* depends largely on reinforcement, and differentiation in self-conception can have important implications for the individual's well-being. Concepts were also said to differ in *salience,* with the degree of salience depending on the amount of training, the stimulus situation, and the motivation at a given moment.

We then returned to the question of consistency, to note that concepts could be compared with respect to their degree of *consistency* with other self-conceptions. Such differences were seen as especially useful in understanding why certain concepts of self are more maleable than others. We finally considered *self-evaluation,* a dimension of cardinal importance in understanding behavior. Concepts vary in their degree of emotional loading, with the learning process investing certain concepts with positive affect and others with negative. Again, the learning process was seen as intimately bound with language training and communication.

We are now ready to ask whether these theoretical statements hold up in light of factual evidence. We shall be able to judge first by studying the impact of the social world on self-conception. Then, in Part IV, we shall see how useful the notion of self-conception is in predicting the behavior of the individual.

III

The Development of Self-Conception

SOCIAL INTERACTION DOES MUCH to furnish the basic repertoire of concepts used by the person to understand himself and to guide his conduct. Still largely unanswered, however, is the question of specialized identity. How does each individual come to view himself in a particular and specialized way—a way that sets him apart from others? An entire culture may draw from the same basic repertoire of concepts in understanding self; however, each person draws from this basic pool in a unique way. In this part we shall explore the central processes involved in determining the individual's conception of himself. In addition, we shall examine one approach to measuring the resulting product—the configuration of self-conception.

One answer to the problem of identity, or individualized self-conception, can be derived from our earlier discussion of conceptual process. The individual may simply *label his dominant behavior patterns* in socially prescribed ways. He might first learn, for instance, that certain behavior is generally classified as "antisocial" and other behavior as "sociable." He then observes that his own behavior falls largely into the former as opposed to the latter category and applies the label accordingly. With continuous confirmation of this label, the concept of "antisocial" should come to play a dominant role in his view of himself. From this standpoint, self-conception may be considered little more than a reflection of the person's preformed patterns of behavior—a byproduct of his daily activities. And, it could be ventured, the individual is always "socially accurate" in his understanding of self. He is simply labelling himself in the same way that others would

40

in light of his particular behavior. Such notions, however, are far too simplistic.

Let us take a close look at several additional processes that play a profound role in fashioning the individual's special notions of who he is.

REFLECTED APPRAISAL AND THE "LOOKING-GLASS" SELF

As early as 1902 the sociologist Charles Horton Cooley developed the theory that one's ideas of self are significantly affected by what he imagines others think of him. Thus, Cooley reasoned, we feel "ashamed to seem evasive in the presence of a straightforward man, cowardly in the presence of a brave one, gross in the eyes of a refined one, and so on. We always imagine, and in imagining share the judgments of the other mind." The result, said Cooley, was a "looking-glass" self, one that reflected the imagined appraisals of others. This theory was later elaborated by George Herbert Mead in 1925. Having a strong empirical bent, Mead was little satisfied with such vague concepts as "imaginings" and attempted to pin the process down more precisely. For Mead the child was said to observe the behavior of "significant others" around him—his mother, father, brothers, and so on and to imitate such behavior in his play. Inasmuch as these others behave in certain ways toward the child, he begins to adopt these orientations toward himself. In Mead's terms he "takes the role of the other." Over time he comes to think of himself in terms of others' behavior toward him. To be treated by one's family as "incapable" is eventually to see one's self in the same way.

When Mead's ideas were later harnessed to scientific methodology, they stimulated considerable activity. Early research attempted to document Mead's notion that self-conception is a reflection of others' views toward self by means of correlational techniques. Subjects of study were typically asked to describe themselves along a number of different dimensions. Their acquaintances (and sometimes specific family members) were then asked to rate them along these same dimensions. Correlations were then computed between the two sets of ratings, with the usual result that subjects' self-ratings were strongly correlated with the ratings of them by others. Unfortunately, such results are not very instructive. They do not demonstrate a sound causal connection between others' views toward self and self-conception. Such correlations could quite well result from the person's conceiving of himself in a specific way and convincing others of this identity.

Much more convincing are experimental studies demonstrating that with a systematic alteration of a person A's overt communication of what he thinks of B, B's self-conception changes accordingly. Videbeck (1960) was one of the first to demonstrate this phenomenon in a direct way. Videbeck studied 30 students in a speech class, each of whom read aloud six poems in the presence of a "visiting expert" in oral communication. At random, and without regard to actual performance, half the subjects received from the expert a positive appraisal. The appraisal informed them particularly of their superiority in controlling voice and conveying meaning. The remaining half of the subjects each received a critical appraisal of the same qualities.

Both before and after the experimental session, subjects made a number of self-ratings. Specifically, they made estimates on a series of nine-point scales of their adequacy in oral communication. These estimates were of three kinds: first, their adequacy in controlling voice and conveying meaning, that is, the attributes specifically appraised by the expert; second, their adequacy in areas related to those appraised but not specifically covered by the expert; and third, unrelated abilities, such as their adequacy in social conversation. If reflected appraisal is important in molding self-conception, subjects receiving the positive evaluations should come to rate themselves as more adequate after the session than before, and subjects receiving the critical appraisals should show a reverse effect. Further, in keeping with our discussion of differentiation in self-conception, the greatest change in self-ratings should be found on items reflecting the content of the appraisals, less should be found in ratings of related abilities, and the least change should be revealed in estimates of unrelated abilities.

Were these expectations confirmed? Figure III-1 exhibits the amount of change in self-ratings as found in each of the content areas. Clearly, the results lend substantial support to the initial propositions. Subjects who received a positive appraisal showed a general increase in their feelings of self-adequacy, an increase that was strongest for attributes directly appraised and weakest for unrelated aspects. Subjects who received a negative appraisal revised their self-estimates in a negative direction, with the impact varying directly with the relevance of the content to the appraisals.

Videbeck's study is important in demonstrating that appraisal reflected from others determines one's conception of self. Since this time, however, the important issue for research has been to determine the conditions under which reflected appraisal is *most* effective. Certainly we don't respond equally to all views that others communicate to us about ourselves.

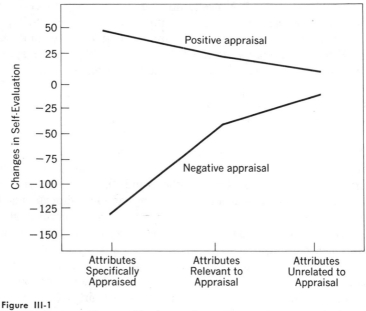

Figure III-1
Self-Evaluation Changes Resulting from Expert Appraisal. (*Adapted from Videbeck, 1960.*)

Under certain conditions we may be shaken to the core by another's appraisal of us; at other times we may react with indifference or even disdain. The problem, then, is to be more exact in specifying which others and what conditions are most influential. From evidence to date, it appears that six factors related to the appraiser and appraisal are most significant.

Characteristics of the Appraiser

Credibility Certain persons seem to be highly knowledgeable about human relations in general or about individuals in particular, and others much less so. When an appraiser appears to have expertise in any given situation, we are more likely to place our trust in his evaluations. In effect, he is more *credible*. Attitude change research has shown that the more credible the communicator, the greater will be his impact on our conception of self. This is only one reason that family members are particularly influential in determining self-conception. If parents communicate to their son that he is "irresponsible," he may well come to see himself in this way; after all, he may tell himself, no one has better knowledge of his behavior. And for the same reason, youth may later reject their parents' views of them. Once they spend the greater part of their time in peer groups, their parents may seem much less "qualified" to make appraisals. We shall turn to evidence related to credibility momentarily.

Personalism   All too often, others communicate things to us without seeming to be truly aware of us as individuals. Their appraisals of us appear insincere, biased to serve their own ends, or the result of lazy disregard for detail. How many times have students accused college administrators of just such impersonalism, while the administrators find the students equally impersonal. On the other hand, there is the communicator who appears to take into account our every action, who attends to the subtleties in our behavior and modifies his appraisal accordingly. This type of communicator may be called *personalistic* and should have a greater influence over our views of self.

One experimental study has attempted to demonstrate such an effect. This study (Gergen, 1965) concentrated on the person's esteem for self. Female subjects were interviewed by an attractive girl a few years senior to them. During the interview it was the subject's task to rate herself along a variety of dimensions. The interviewer subtly showed signs of agreement whenever the subject rated herself positively and signs of disagreement whenever the subject rated herself negatively. Agreement was signalled by smiles, nods, and an occasional brief statement such as, "Yes, I think so too." Disagreement was expressed by silence, frowns, and occasional verbal statements. Prior to the interview, half the subjects were instructed that the interviewer would simply be practicing a set of interview techniques and that all her behavior was prescribed for her (impersonal condition). The remaining half of the subjects were told that the interviewer had few instructions as to her behavior and that it was her main task to be as honest as possible during the interview (personalistic condition). Both before and after the interview all subjects were given a test of self-esteem and told to evaluate themselves as honestly as possible.

The results of the study showed that subjects who received the impersonal appraisals showed little increase in self-esteem as a result of the interview. On the other hand, subjects who received the personalistic appraisals showed a strong increase in self-esteem—a difference exceeding that found in a control group interviewed without reflected appraisal. In other words, persons are more strongly affected when others appear sincere, uncalculated, and attuned to them as individuals.

Characteristics of the Appraisal

Discrepancy between appraisal and self-view   In addition to the characteristics of the appraiser, the appraisals we receive from others may also vary in a number of respects. One of the most interesting is the extent to which the appraisal differs from the person's self-conception at the moment. Some people see us much as we see ourselves, while others disagree markedly with our self-opinions. A person feels he is only "average," for example, in his ability to play the guitar. One friend says that he is better than average. A second friend informs him that he is among the best he has heard. Which friend is more likely to change the individual's estimate of his ability? One appraisal differs only slightly from the individual's self-estimate; the other is highly *discrepant*. The extent of this discrepancy between another's view and our own can make a great deal of difference in how much our self-estimate is affected.

As the discrepancy between self-concept and the other's appraisal increases, two effects are produced which seem to work in opposite directions. On the one hand, as the discrepancy is increased, so is the pressure to change one's concept of self. If you consider yourself "very friendly," there is simply less pressure to alter this view if another says that you appear to be "moderately friendly" than if he says you are a "rather cold" person. The latter appraisal is more likely to cause you to scan your own behavior for evidence that might have led him to this conclusion. Finding at least some confirmations for his view, you are more likely to revise your own estimate of self in the direction of the appraisal.

On the other hand, as the other's appraisal becomes increasingly discrepant from your own, it may appear less and less accurate. If you see yourself as "very honest," and someone says you are "one of the most dishonest persons he has ever met," you may pay little attention to him. More likely, you will question his power of discernment.

Faced with these opposing tendencies, other factors may be crucial in determining which is decisive. One prime factor that may tip the balance at this point is the credibility of the communicator. If the communicator appears to be a highly credible source, we are less likely to question his accuracy and thus more likely to reappraise ourselves as his views become more discrepant from our own. But if the communicator seems to lack knowledge or expertise, the greater the discrepancy between his view and our own, the less likely we are to take his view seriously.

This reasoning is nicely validated in a study carried out by Bergin in 1962. Half the subjects were exposed to a highly credible source whose view of them differed from their own by either a low, medium, or high degree. In this condition the subjects (all college students) reported to the medical school for a personality assessment procedure. The room was filled with medical equipment, books, and a portrait of Freud. The "director of the project" informed the subjects that he wished to compare the subject's self-ratings with other measures that were more reliable and objective. Each subject then filled out a number of measures, among which was a self-rating of his masculinity. After several days he returned and was told that the estimate he made of his masculinity differed from that found on the "more objective" measure of the trait. In the low-discrepancy conditions, subjects were told that there was only a two-point difference (of a possible 13) between their self-estimates and those found on the other instrument; subjects in the medium-discrepancy condition were informed that the difference was four points; high-discrepancy subjects found a six-point difference to exist between the two measures. Since there appeared to be a good reason for it, subjects were then asked to complete the self-ratings a second time.

The other half of the subjects in the experiment encountered a much different situation—one designed to create the impression that the source of the appraisal was low in credibility. In contrast to the scientific atmosphere used to create high credibility, testing was carried out in a dingy room. When the subject returned the second time, he was rated on a number of dimensions by a high school student, as "part of a study in social perception." Just as in the first case, one third of the subjects found the student's estimates differed by only two points from their own, one third found a difference of four points, and one third, a difference of six points. Subjects then rated themselves a second time. In this experiment as in most others where falsification is used, subjects were fully informed of the procedure and rationale at the termination of the session.

The major focus of the study was on the amount of change in self-ratings produced by the various types of appraisals. Self-rating change for subjects in each of the six conditions is depicted in Figure III-2. The results are clear: When the source is highly credible, his effect on self-conception becomes greater as his appraisal is increasingly discrepant from the subject's initial self-estimate. But when his credibility is low, he has less and less effect as his views become more extreme. In the case of high credibility one might think of a psychiatrist who wishes his patient to see himself differently, perhaps more accurately. These results suggest that the psychiatrist will have a greater impact on the patient by taking a position that sharply contrasts with the patient's initial view of himself. One must be somewhat cautious, however, because it also appears that if the

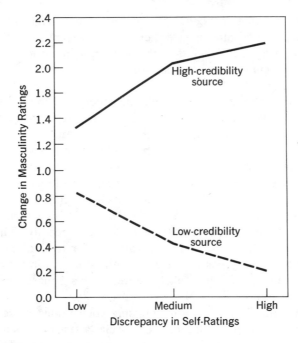

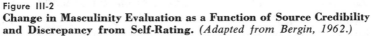

Figure III-2
Change in Masculinity Evaluation as a Function of Source Credibility and Discrepancy from Self-Rating. *(Adapted from Bergin, 1962.)*

appraisal becomes too extreme, it might reinstigate the patient's feelings that it is not reliable.

Number of confirmations   One may criticize the various studies described thus far because of their non-continuous character. They take only a short time, provide the subject with only a single appraisal of himself, and measure his self-estimate soon afterward. Can we expect such procedures to create truly lasting changes in self-conception? Decidedly not. Such studies are intended only to confirm that certain processes operate in specified ways. The ultimate significance of the findings rests on an additional assumption: the greater the number of confirmations of a given appraisal, the greater its salience on any future occasion. Thus, if a credible and personalistic source appraises us daily in a way that differs greatly from our own, the effects on us could be profound. This is another reason that the views communicated by parents to their children are likely to have such long-term effects. With continuous, long-term exposure to a particular appraisal, the person's relevant view of self may be determined for life—strongly resistent to change if not immutable. Thus we find many adults whose accomplishments give them every reason to feel "strong" and "able" and who are nevertheless constantly haunted by a voice from the past reminding them of their inadequacies.

Consistency of confirmations   In order to understand the impact of long-term appraisals, we must take into account not only the number of appraisals but also their consistency with other communications the person receives about himself. A person may hear a hundred times that he is "normal," but if each of these appraisals is matched by another indicating "abnormality," the effects of the initial communication may be negated. However, as we saw in Part II, it is quite possible to hold inconsistent views of self. If one's teacher views him as "witless" and his summer employer as "brilliant," both aspects may be learned quite readily. The fact that the communicator, the time, and the location differ renders one less sensitive to the inconsistency. As we have seen, the situation in which we learn a certain conception of self is likely to recall this conception on similar occasions in the future.

The case in which we learn opposing conceptions of self from the *same* individual may be singled out for special attention. Such a situation has been termed a *double-bind* and may take place frequently and subtly in social life. A hug that is at the same time painful, a slap on the back that also knocks the wind out of us, or a gift that defies common sense of taste, all communicate that we are at once valued and valueless. At least one group of theorists (Bateson, *et al.,* 1956) have even maintained that the confusion and stress resulting from a prolonged double-bind in childhood may give rise to schizophrenia.

The extent to which the consistency of appraisals affects our capacity to incorporate them will also depend on the functional value of the concepts involved and on the extent to which we are trained to avoid inconsistencies. We shall soon have a closer look at the effects of this latter factor.

Evaluative connotation   Findings from a variety of sources all seem to indicate that appraisals which are positive in *evaluative connotation* are more rapidly learned and less quickly forgotten than negative appraisals. We are hungry for compliments but sceptical of criticism. Evidence supporting this proposition comes primarily from research on the learning and memory of material relevant to one's beliefs. Such studies consistently show that facts or opinions coinciding with one's beliefs or supporting one's values tend to be learned more rapidly and forgotten more slowly. Although there is no direct evidence as yet regarding self-conception, there is every reason to suspect that the same process is effective in this case, as we shall see when we deal with the effects of motivation on self-conception.

In summary, reflected appraisal may have a powerful effect on the person's concept of self. However, the strength of this effect may vary markedly. It should be maximal when (1) the appraiser is credible and personalistic in his approach; (2) he advocates great change in self-conception and he does it often; (3) his appraisal is not contradicted by other information; and (4) his appraisal is a positive one.

SOCIAL COMPARISON: DEFINING SELF IN RELATION TO OTHERS

Considering the effects of reflected appraisal alone, we arrive at a rather dismaying picture of man. He seems only a passive agent mirroring the opinions of others; identity becomes a mere reflection of the faces around him. In order to expand this picture, we must now attend to the effects of social comparison on the individual's conception of himself.

The early social theorist Thorstein Veblen was intrigued by the question of why people seem so bent on accumulating goods and property beyond their physical needs. He was struck by what seemed to be a close association in industrialized culture between one's self-esteem and his accumulated possessions. Self-esteem did not seem to depend on the absolute amount accumulated, but rather on the amount one had *in comparison with others*. "The end sought by accumulation is to rank high in comparison with the rest of the community. . . . So long as the comparison is distinctly unfavorable to himself, the normal, average individual will live in chronic dissatisfaction" (p. 42).

The understanding of social comparison effects was much improved, however, with the publication in 1954 of Leon Festinger's, "A Theory of Social Comparison Processes." In this article Festinger argued that people have a continuous need to establish the correctness of their beliefs and attitudes. When there is little valid, factual evidence on which to rely, they turn to others. Specifically, they compare their own beliefs and attitudes about the world with those held by others in order to assess the validity of their own position. This reasoning has obvious implications for the development of self-conception. If asked if he is "healthy," the person may simply rely on the factual data provided by monitoring his own feelings of well-being; little in the way of comparison need take place. On the other hand, if he is unsure whether to consider himself "dull," "religious," "lovable," or "idealistic," he may depend in large measure on how he sees himself in comparison with others.

The effects of comparison on self-conception have been demonstrated in an experiment carried out by Morse and Gergen (in press). This study is particularly worth our attention because it is one of the few that has also shown how individual differences in consistency orientation affect changes in self-conception. Subjects were students at the University of Michigan who answered an advertisement for part-time jobs in the research institute. When a subject arrived for the application procedure, he was seated in a room by himself and given a number of self-rating forms to fill out. One of these forms was especially designed to assess individual differences in consistency level (Gergen & Morse, 1967). Subjects scoring high on the measure could be characterized as having very inconsistent concepts of self; low scorers would see their various aspects of self as highly consistent. A second measure given to the subjects assessed their generalized evaluation of self or *self-esteem.*

After each subject had completed these measures, the secretary entered the room, bringing with her another "applicant" for the part-time work who was, in fact, an experimental collaborator. For half the subjects he appeared to be socially desirable; he wore a dark business suit and carried an attaché case. Upon being seated, he opened the case to remove several sharpened pencils, revealing copies of a statistics book and a philosophy text. This applicant we can name *Mr. Clean.* The remaining half of the subjects met *Mr. Dirty,* who wore a smelly sweat shirt and no socks and appeared generally dazed by the entire procedure. When he was seated he tossed onto the table his worn copy of *The Carpetbaggers.* After several minutes in the presence of one of these two applicants, the subject was given additional forms to complete. One of these was a second measure of self-esteem.

The experimental question was whether the mere presence of the stimulus person would cause a shift in the subject's self-esteem level. If the comparison process was at play, Mr. Clean should cause subjects to feel less positive about themselves—lacking in many desirable attributes. Self-esteem should decrease. Mr. Dirty should create just the opposite effect, for in comparison with him subjects should feel more secure about themselves. It was further hypothesized that differences in consistency orientation would also affect the degree of self-esteem change. Specifically, it was reasoned that subjects who were inconsistent as measured by the scale would be more apt to shift in self-esteem level. They should be more flexible in accepting different ways of viewing themselves. Consistent subjects, it was felt, would be less able to incorporate new and potentially inconsistent information into their coherent self-view.

The results of the experiment are featured in Figure III-3, where

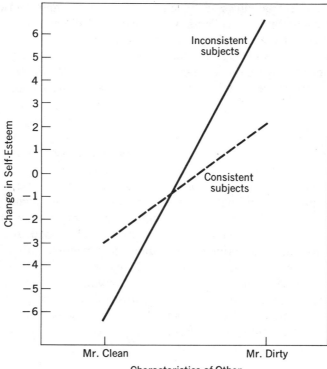

Figure III-3
**Changes in Self-Esteem as a Function of the Other's Characteristics
and Level of Self-Consistency.** *(From Morse & Gergen, in press.)*

mean change in self-esteem has been charted for both high and low consistency subjects exposed to Mr. Clean or Mr. Dirty. When Mr. Clean was
present, there was a tendency for all subjects to experience a decrease in
self-esteem. Also supporting our earlier reasoning, Mr. Dirty produced
just the opposite effect. Differences resulting from level of self-consistency
were also revealed. Subjects characterized by high inconsistency in their
self-view were more susceptible to the effects of social comparison. To a
greater extent than consistent subjects, they saw themselves more negatively
in Mr. Clean's presence and more positively when confronted by Mr.
Dirty.

Such findings have broad implications. We have already discussed
the significance that high self-esteem may have for one's mental well-being.
These results suggest that one's level of self-regard may be vitally affected

by the social surroundings in which he happens to find himself. Low-ranking students at elite colleges and universities often suffer a life-long blow to their esteem; had they attended an average institution, such pain might have been avoided. Similarly, the lower-class child living in or near a middle-class neighborhood and the rural housewife whose husband's change of jobs places her in the midst of urban sophistication may also suffer.

We must add to this picture another type of social comparison which often shapes the individual's identity. Cooley (1922) spoke of the problems of men with great ambition who do not depend on others for corroboration of their capacities. Instead they harden "themselves against immediate influences, enduring or repressing the pains of present depreciation, and cultivating in imagination the approval of some higher tribune." The major lesson of Cooley's discussion is that persons may, over time, develop *internalized standards of comparison.* Childhood socialization, religious training, and primary education, for example, all attempt to implant in the child standards that may thereafter allow him to determine when he is "good," when he has "sinned," or when he is "correct." The more intensive the learning of such standards, the less susceptible the person may be to either reflected appraisal or comparisons in the immediate situation. Unfortunately, such learning may also reduce the person's capacity to adapt to new and changing circumstances.

MOTIVATION AND BIASED SCANNING

During the normal course of development, the person learns to seek a variety of ends—the approval or dominance of others, the accumulation of resources, a feeling of peace, and so on. Most psychologists look upon these motives as learned through social conditioning and subject to wide variation from person to person. A certain class of these learned motives may be termed *identity aspirations.* We all learn to seek certain ways of being identified—from wanting to be "good" when a child, or "popular" as an adolescent, to wanting to be "a doctor" as an adult. At these times it may be gratifying to conceptualize self in these ways. The justification for applying these concepts to self usually lies in the opinion of others. If our behavior measures up to the socially accepted definition of "good," "popular," or "a doctor," our identity has been confirmed.

Yet, the identities to which we aspire may be affected by factors other than social confirmation. Of particular importance are the effects that aspirations themselves may have. Aspiring toward a certain identity may help us to reach that state subjectively, even when objective confirmation is lacking. We may come to believe we are something simply because we wish to be. In essence, motives themselves may influence self-conception. How does this take place?

In determining whether one's behavior meets certain judgmental standards, it is necessary to scan both the environment and one's memory for instances of confirmation or disconfirmation. The child may search the facial expression of his mother for cues enabling him to think of himself as "good" or the adolescent girl may be sensitive to the number of times she is asked out to determine whether she is "popular." In addition to the environment, the person also scans his memory. The doctor continues to think of himself as a doctor even when he is not in his office giving treatment; his memory provides continuous confirmation of his position. And yet, in numerous instances the information we glean from the environment and our memory is confused and contradictory. Can the child be sure that the mother's smile signifies that he is "good," or is she silently chuckling over his ineptness? And in assessing her popularity, the adolescent may remember last week's companions as well as last month's solitude.

When the circumstances for confirming one's identity are ambiguous, one's motives may have a strong impact on which cues are selected for consideration. Specifically, there is a strong tendency to select out those cues that provide positive confirmation—that is, gratify one's aspirations. The reason for this bias seems to stem from basic patterns of searching for gratification established in early childhood. If a child is hungry he searches for a substance that will gratify his hunger; if he is in pain, he searches for a behavior that will end the pain. In essence, the search selects objects or events that gratify and avoids or dismisses those which do not. In terms of identity, the individual who desires to see himself a certain way should thus be more sensitive to cues that confirm this desire than to those which do not. He should attend more closely to those events which might serve as exemplars of the desired self-concept; failures of confirmation are painful and thus avoided. Perceptual scanning is biased, then, toward seeing ourselves as we wish to be.

There is abundant evidence supporting such reasoning. First, with respect to scanning the environment, an early study by Pepitone (1950) varied the motivation of high school students to receive tickets for a basketball game. He then observed the effects of motivation on their perception of judges who decided the distribution of the tickets. Half the high school student subjects were told that the tickets were for a highly touted college game, while the other half were offered tickets for a high school game of little note. To receive the tickets they had to be approved by a panel of judges who would talk to them about various aspects of the sport. By prearrangement, one of the judges was consistently more friendly than the other two. After the interview, subjects rated both how friendly and how influential in determining the winners each judge was. The results showed that subjects highly motivated to win the tickets rated the friendly judge as more friendly and more influential than subjects in the low motivation condition. When they most desired the tickets they sought cues in the situation that would help to fulfill their desires. More highly controlled studies (for example, Rosen, 1954; Eriksen & Browne, 1956) have shown that people recognize less readily those stimuli in a perceptual task that have previously been associated with pain produced by electrical shock. However, when shock can be avoided by noticing the appearance of a particular stimulus, the stimulus is more rapidly recognized. The rapidity of recognition, then, depends on whether the recognition is gratifying.

Research has also shown a strong tendency for persons to learn more rapidly and forget more slowly facts that are self-gratifying. In an early study by Levine and Murphy (1943) anti-Communists more efficiently learned and less readily forgot anti-Communist statements than pro-Communist ones; for pro-Communist subjects exactly the reverse was true. Later, Taft (1954) demonstrated that Negroes were better able than white subjects to remember material sympathetic to Negroes both immediately after a learning experience and again several days later. Canon (1964) and Jones & Aneshansel (1956) have also shown that information useful for achieving success in an argument is more accurately retained; people may even learn an opponent's arguments more rapidly if victory is secured by doing so. In short, the scanning of both the environment and memory is biased toward self-gratification.

One note of caution is necessary in the interpretation of the research findings in this domain. While the research illustrates that biases occur, the precise processes underlying this tendency are not clearly understood. Several other processes could also produce the research results discussed thus far; account of these is provided elsewhere (Gergen, in press). The problems for future research are two in number: to isolate the exact processes that create these scanning patterns and to demonstrate that they operate in the same way with identity aspirations as they do with other motives.

ROLE PLAYING: IDENTITY AND THE DRAMA OF DAILY LIFE

The similarities between dramatic acting and the behavior of persons in their daily lives has been apparent to social commentators for many centuries. Just as the actor learns to recite his lines on cue, so in daily life we learn the behavior and words that are appropriate for each occasion. The term *role* is commonly used by both the theatre and the social sciences to refer to these specified patterns of behavior.

One phenomenon that has been noted by actors, and more recently by social scientists, is a peculiar tendency for the person to identify with the role he is required to play. "Identification" in this case means, first, that the person comes to see himself as actually having those attributes characterizing the role and, second, that he tends to adopt the role behavior for use in situations where the behavior is not strictly required. In short, the person comes to develop an identity based on the role and to use this identity in his behavior over a wide variety of circumstances. In an unpublished study by Gergen and Preiss, over 70 percent of a large group of actors, ranging from unskilled amateurs to trained professionals, indicated they had experienced this carry-over from their stage roles to their off-stage lives.

Social theorists have also noted the effects of roles on personality. In discussing the effects of teaching on teachers, Waller (1932) once commented,

> That stiff and formal manner into which the young teacher compresses himself every morning when he puts on his collar becomes . . . a plaster cast which at length he cannot loosen. . . .: The didactic manner, the authoritative manner, the flat, assured tones of voice that go with them, are bred in the teacher by his dealings in the classroom . . . and these traits are carried over by the teacher into his personal relations.

Merton (1940) has also discussed how the role of the bureaucrat, with its emphasis on strict conformity to standards, causes the role player to become timid and conservative.

Only within the past two decades has careful study been carried out on this phenomenon. The bulk of this work falls into the attitude change tradition, where investigators have been concerned with factors that cause people to change their attitudes about events or persons in their environment. Since attitudes can be viewed as conceptual statements with heavy evaluative connotations, such work has clear relevance to the problem of self-conception. Factors that change our views of others should also operate to change our views of self. One of the ground-breaking studies in this area was carried out by Janis and King in 1954. Subjects in this experiment were asked to present an extemporaneous talk favoring a particular position (for example, that a cure for the common cold would soon be found). The talk was to be built around a set of supporting arguments provided by the experimenter. Each subject in the group was required to give such a talk and to listen to the talks of two other subjects on different issues. Attitudes toward each of the issues were assessed both before and after the talks had been given. The results showed strong differences between attitude change when one had given a talk himself and when he had listened to another. Subjects changed far more toward the position they themselves had advocated than toward the positions they heard others advocate. Playing the role, then, seemed to move the person's underlying view in the direction favored by the role.

The findings of Janis and King have been criticized on a number of counts, and many more exacting studies have been carried out since then. Much of this research has attempted to isolate conditions under which role playing will have maximal effects, with much attending argument as to exactly why role playing creates the effects it does (see Elms, 1969). Although the research is far from complete at this time, it seems clear that several different processes are simultaneously at work in producing role-playing effects. In discussing these various processes we can gain an understanding of the conditions under which role playing is most powerful in its effects on identity.

Memory Scanning

In many role-playing experiments subjects are required to develop a set of arguments in support of a particular position. Such circumstances are optimal for setting in motion the biased scanning of memory discussed in the preceding section. That is, the subject is motivated to seek arguments that support his position and is less likely to be sensitized to opposing arguments. With the increased salience of the biased set of arguments, his private views should be affected in the direction of the role he is to present. For example, if a person applies for a job he might wish to present himself as "confident" and "mature." During the job interview he might scan his memory in search of positive exemplars of these concepts, avoiding those which are inappropriate. He might remember the debating prize he won, his good marks in school, and his success in coping with difficult situations. The increased salience of these confirmations should be sufficient to cause him to believe, at least for the moment, that he is indeed "confident" and "mature." In the same way, an athlete might boost his confidence while preparing for an athletic contest, or a civil rights advocate come to see himself as more "extreme" or "liberal" through public demonstrations.

Some evidence supporting this interpretation of role-playing effects is found in a study by Gergen and Taylor (1966). In this study subjects spent ten minutes in planning a talk they were to give on why they were qualified for a particular position. Both some weeks before the experiment and immediately after, subjects filled out a measure of self-esteem with instructions to be as honest as possible in their self-assessments. A control group completed similar forms but did not go through the exercise of developing the talk. A comparison of self-esteem change in the two groups showed that the former underwent far greater change than the latter. The simple process of scanning the memory for supportive facts proved sufficient to alter self-conception within the situation.

It should be noted here that the effects of memory scanning can occur without the added necessity of carrying out the role; actual role behavior is unnecessary. In this sense, we can speak in terms of *implicit role playing*—the internal or cognitive placement of oneself into a role category.

The Effects of Reward and Punishment

In the acting out of roles there are numerous rewards and punishments that may become associated with the concept of self presented in any role. As we saw in our earlier discussion of the evaluative weighting of concepts, rewards and punishments associated with a concept affect the evaluative connotation of the concept. Thus, if a person is rewarded for behaving in a particular role, he should come to prefer it and should receive gratification for thinking of himself in terms of the role. In order to gain a better understanding of this process, we might consider four prominent sources of reward or punishment.

Others' evaluations   As an early study by Scott (1959) demonstrated, when others respond positively to the presentation of a role, the role player is more likely to change his attitude in the direction of his presentation. Thus, the man who is praised for his work is the man who will soon become identified with it. It should be noted, however, that while approval produces identification, disapproval does not necessarily produce the reverse. Under certain conditions, disapproval may only cause the person to identify even more closely with his behavior (see Cohen, 1959), scanning his memory for additional support or intensifying his behavior. If a person who considers himself a leader is told he is incapable of leading, he may increase his attempts to lead, thereby increasing his identification with his desired role.

It is also possible that *actual* approval may sometimes be unnecessary. As Cooley (1922) reasoned, it is sufficient if the person simply imagines that others approve or disapprove. It is unnecessary for the girl who dons a new dress to receive the direct approval of others for her to think of herself as "chic" or "beautiful." The imagined compliments, stimulated by her familiarity with the evaluations in the mass media, may be sufficient to boost her self-confidence.

Own evaluation of the role   Most often the roles that we play have some evaluative weighting attached to them at the very outset. For instance, a man faced with the prospect of military draft typically has strong feelings about the role for which he has been selected. These preliminary evaluations may have a strong effect on the rapidity with which role identification takes place, with more positively evaluated roles adopted more rapidly. Most interesting, however, are cases in which persons are induced to play roles they dislike. Janis and Mann (1965), for example, had smokers play the role of a patient who receives the news from his physician that he has lung cancer. This role proved sufficiently traumatic that it not only altered attitudes about smoking, but brought about a significant reduction in cigarette consumption as long as two weeks after the experience. Devaluation of the role thus produced counter-identification.

Incentives   A person may be offered varying incentives for playing a particular role. Financial gain, prestige, social conscience, and family approval are all incentives that may push the individual into one occupational role rather than another. The greater the reward he is offered, the more rapidly should role identification take place. Evidence supporting this view is found in two studies. Rosenberg (1965) found that the greater the amount of money students were paid to write an essay supporting an unpopular position taken by the university administration, the more they changed their attitudes to support the administration. Carlsmith, Collins, & Helmreich (1966) paid subjects varying amounts for writing a statement to convince others that an obviously dull task was really very interesting. Under certain conditions, they found that the greater the pay, the more attitudes changed. In essence, if a person is paid enough to lie he may come to believe in his lies. It should be noted that incentives may have a double impact, not only operating as rewards attached to various concepts, but also invigorating one's memory scanning. However, we shall find that the impact of incentives is not always so easily predictable.

Task difficulty   It is easier to adopt the behavior required by some roles than by others. We may be quite familiar with the role of "father" and find little difficulty acting within this role when the time comes, while the role of "lawyer" may be quite difficult for the fledgling lawyer. In spite of all his training in modern teaching practices, a young teacher's first classroom presentations may very likely reproduce those of his old teachers—it is easier to fall back on the old roles than to adopt new ones. Role difficulty is, of course, a form of punishment and as such may inhibit rapid identification with a role. Support for this argument is found in an experiment conducted by Jansen and Stolurow (1962). Psychiatric aides in a mental hospital practiced a number of roles in order to improve their interpersonal skills on the job. Here it was found that the less difficult the roles assigned, the greater the impact of the experience on the aides. Again, however, we must not be absolute, in light of other findings on this problem.

Dissonance Reduction

In addition to memory scanning and reinforcement effects, the person's desire to maintain consistency among his concepts of himself may also affect the results of role playing. As we discussed in Part II, the person may learn from an early age to avoid inconsistent notions about who he is and confrontations with inconsistent concepts of self may become noxious to him. Festinger (1957) and others have shown that people generally attempt to reduce such "dissonance" whenever it occurs. The greater the dissonance, the stronger the attempt to reduce it.

This line of reasoning is clearly relevant to situations in which a person plays a role that is discrepant with his conception of self. If he normally defines himself as an "atheist" and finds himself appealing to a divine power in a time of a crisis, he may experience dissonance. As Brehm (1960) has reasoned, dissonance reduction should cause this person to alter his thought about himself in the direction of seeing himself as more "religious." Since his "religious" *behavior* is apparent and irrevocable, he should reduce dissonance by modifying his *ideas* about himself.

Although this reasoning is quite sound, some of its consequences are directly opposed to what we have said thus far. First, from the dissonance perspective, the greater the incentive for adopting a given role, the less should be the resulting change in conception. If a person is offered a great deal of money for behaving in a certain way he should be less likely to see his behavior as violating self-conception. After all, he might reason, he is playing the part simply for the money and the behavior has no relevance to him personally. Such a prediction is precisely the reverse of what we said above concerning reinforcement. Several investigators (Festinger & Carlsmith, 1959; Carlsmith, Collins, & Helmreich, 1966) have demonstrated that under certain conditions a person will be more likely to shift his private position toward his public stance when the incentive is less. Task difficulty creates a similar problem. If a person finds a role-playing task very difficult, he has a greater problem in justifying his behavior to himself. In effect, greater dissonance is created and the result should be more identification with the role rather than less, as reasoned above. Zimbardo (1965) has also found experimental support for this dissonance prediction.

At this point it is too early to reach a conclusion about the conditions under which reinforcement as opposed to dissonance effects will be found in role-playing situations. Our earlier discussion of conditions under which dissonance reduction might be most operative is obviously relevant. Greater clarification is needed also on precisely how dissonance reduction takes place. It may be that its effects are primarily due to memory scanning as discussed earlier. Thus, a person may experience dissonance (or conflict) when playing a role that seems alien to him. However, when little reward is offered for adopting this role or when great effort is required, the person may be influenced to scan his memory more diligently for reasons to support this otherwise alien activity. If a top administrator is asked to resign and is offered little reward for doing what is for him a very difficult thing, he might be inclined to think up reasons to justify his doing so. He might recall his mistakes as leader, the great difficulty of the job, or his yearnings for the comfort of retirement, and then more readily accept the new role. In this biased scanning of memory, he may convince himself that stepping down is appropriate. Future research may help to shed light on this issue.

Labelling of Role Behavior

Finally, role-playing effects may be due to the person's *labelling* of his overt behavior at the moment. If induced to play a given role, the person simultaneously observes himself acting in a certain way. These actions confirm or reinforce certain concepts of self. If the individual sees himself acting like a "militant," his thoughts about himself must subsequently include this behavior. Such a process requires the actual performance of role behavior in order to be effective.

In summary, there are at least four different processes that may cause role playing to affect self-conception, and each suggests certain elements that might increase or decrease these effects in any given situation. To the extent that memory scanning is at work, role-playing effects should be increased if there is time for cognitive work to take place and if the role is a positively valued one. Reinforcement effects, as we have seen, may be enhanced by a variety of factors such as positive reactions to the role by others, playing a positive role, and so on. Dissonance effects should be enhanced when the role is difficult to play and the incentives are low. The process of behavior labelling should be enhanced by having verbal labels readily available and behavior entirely consistent with these labels. For example, the rapidity with which a humble and struggling young author changes his view of himself to "leader of the avant garde" after the success of his first novel will depend on whether he can call forth from his memory support for this new view, on how much he values the role of "avant garde leader," how much praise he receives, how difficult it is for him to go through the motions required by the role, how much reward is offered, on whether he can recognize his behavior as that of avant garde leader, and on how consistent the new view is with his other conceptions of self. If these factors are favorable, soon the practice of "seeming" will generate "being."

THE CONFIGURATION OF SELF-CONCEPTION

Thus far we have discussed four separate processes that contribute to the development of self-conception: labelling of dominant behavior patterns, reflected appraisal, social comparison, and biased scanning. Role playing may also be included as a fifth, but its effects are best viewed as dependent on the more basic processes just described. It is time now to consider how we can describe the configurations of self-conception that result from these processes.

The answer to this question depends largely on the availability of a suitable measuring device. The problem of developing a measure that is sensitive to all of the various aspects of self-conception discussed in Part II is an extremely complex one, and it is quite clear that much more research will be required before a final solution is reached. The most elaborate and sensitive device that has been developed thus far can be attributed to Chad Gordon (1968). The basis of Gordon's measure is a simple one. The individual is placed in a situation that is as emotionally neutral as possible and asked to write down a list of answers to the question "Who am I?" He is further asked not to be concerned with the logic or importance of his answers and to write as if he were answering only to himself and not to someone else. The respondent may also be asked to rate the importance of each of his responses. The resulting list of responses (typically limited to 15) is then subjected to a sophisticated computer analysis in which each response is first coded into one or more of some 30 content categories.

Then the responses are coded again with respect to evaluative weighting to yield a total self-evaluation score. The category system was developed through extensive research and attempts to include all responses that people normally make.

How do persons describe themselves on this measure? Essentially, there are two broad content categories into which most responses fall. First, there are terms that denote one's membership in various formal or informal groups in society. Here are included one's sex, racial or national heritage, religion, kinship roles, occupational roles, political affiliation, social status, and so on. There is a strong tendency on the part of respondents to describe themselves first with these categories—as if to give themselves specific placement within the society at large. Such terms identify a person by separating him from large segments of society and placing him within smaller subsegments.

The second large group includes conceptual terms that are more personal in nature and that usually denote specific attributes of the individual. Here are included his feelings of competence (or lack of it), descriptions of bodily attributes, ways of relating to other persons, psychological characteristics, intellectual concerns, sense of moral worth (for example, "trustworthy," "responsible"), sense of self-determination ("ambitious," "hardworking"), personal taste ("a jazz fan," "a person who loves nature") and others' feelings toward him ("loved," "respected"). Personal descriptions are typically placed later in the sequence. Once the person has located himself with respect to society at large, these personal terms seem to single him out within his particular social grouping.

Approximately 40–70 percent of the concepts used by respondents have obvious evaluative overtones. The more normal the subject population (for example, college students as compared with institutionalized schizophrenics) the smaller the proportion of evaluative concepts—a finding that may reflect a tendency on the part of college students to respond more defensively on tests of this variety. More importantly, the test shows clear differences between subject populations in generalized self-esteem (the mean evaluative rating for all relevant responses). Among those groups tested so far, the highest self-esteem is found in college populations. Lowest self-esteem is found in groups of alcoholic patients. Alcoholics typically describe themselves in such terms as "I am nothing," "a nobody," "cruel," and "foolish." This finding coincides with much clinical evidence suggesting that alcohol is used by this group as a means of enhancing their otherwise impoverished state of self-esteem.

The ratings made of the importance (roughly equivalent to the "functional value" discussed earlier) of each of the self-concepts are of additional interest. Although the sample on which these results are based (Harvard and Radcliffe students) is in no way representative, it is intriguing to note among the 30 types of concepts used by the students three of the most important are competence, occupational role, and others' feelings toward self. Judging from the importance placed on competence and occupational role, it seems that the university atmosphere, heavy in its emphasis on competition and career training, has a marked effect. The importance attached to others' feelings toward self underscores our earlier discussion of the centrality of self-esteem and its strong dependence on the reactions of others. More surprising, these data show that among the least important concepts to these students were their religious and political affiliations. Social theorists have often seen these attributes as being central to the operation of society. This may be so, but apparently not for the younger and more sophisticated members of society.

Although a measure such as this one can be extremely useful, the major task remains of relating responses on the measure directly with the formative processes described earlier. It is clear that the measure reflects differences in socialization. Not only are there vast differences in responses among individuals, but differences among groups in society have also been found. A comparison of Harvard-Radcliffe students with students at Los Angeles City College, for instance, shows the latter group as more likely to define themselves in terms of an occupational role and less likely to see themselves in terms of student roles and intellectual pursuits. Such differences may well reflect differences in the emphases of the two institutions. However, more precise connections between responses on the measure and developmental processes are needed to clarify such differences.

Further research is also needed to account for other factors. For one, both the testing situation and experiences immediately preceding it may increase the salience of certain concepts that might otherwise be low in salience. If the test is seen to be "psychological" in nature, certain concepts of self (for example, "depressed," "a man of sound mind," "someone who feels inferior") may come to mind. Such concepts would not be salient if the test were seen as sociological, political, religious, or economic in character. The identity of the tester, the test format, or the site may all affect self-perception. As Block (1952) has shown, when respondents are asked to describe themselves as they are with various other individuals (close friend, employer, and so forth) more than 50 percent of their responses are situation-specific—that is, not common across the various situations.

The individual's recent experiences may also distort response patterns. For example, there is little mistaking what was on the mind of a teenager who responded that she was "attractive," "shapely," "five feet four," "not a virgin anymore," and that she "knows how it feels to have loved and lost" (Gordon, 1968). This is not to doubt the importance of these concepts to the girl but rather to point to the fact that her romantic concerns of the moment dominate a third of the responses, to the exclusion of other, more representative possibilities.

In addition, we know very well that people in testing situations often distort their responses to create specific effects. As we shall see in discussing self-presentation, people modify their overt representations of self to gain specific ends in a situation. The extent to which the "Who am I?" format elicits those concepts most generally salient to the person, as opposed to those coined for specific situations, is unknown. This may be an especially important factor to consider since it is known that on most psychological tests people attempt to appear in a positive light (Crowne & Marlowe, 1964) and shield their shortcomings. Future research should do much to solve these types of problems.

SUMMARY

In this part we have discussed the major processes involved in fashioning the individual's specialized conception of self. We saw first that the person could develop concepts of himself by simply labelling his dominant behavior patterns. Second, it was shown that the appraisals received from others could be particularly powerful in molding self-conception. The extent of this influence, however, was seen to depend on the precise characteristics of both the appraiser and his appraisal. Social comparison was viewed as a third major process. It was shown that the person's conception of self depends to an important degree on how he sees himself in relation to others. The scanning of the environment, as biased by motivational pursuits, was also found to play a part in creating the individual's identity. It was seen how the person selectively chooses from his environment and from his memory information that confirms his major aspirations. Finally, role playing was seen to be important in forming self-conception, although the underlying processes and factors that might increase or reduce role-playing effects are still matters of deliberation. After exploring the forces at work in self-development, we took a brief look at one method for assessing the resulting structure of self-conception. The "Who am I?" format was seen to be a valuable tool, but in need of additional investigation to be conclusive.

IV

The Self and
Interpersonal Behavior

*T*HE TRUE SIGNIFICANCE OF ANY THEORY in the social sciences depends on its capacity to predict human behavior. In this part we shall explore several ways in which self-conception is integral to understanding and predicting the course of daily life. First, we shall deal with the core of human relations, the emotions, and see how self-conception is related to our feelings toward others. We shall then move to a second but equally important issue in social life, power and influence. In particular, we shall ask how self-conception influences the division of power in a relationship—who is more likely to initiate influence, who is more likely to be influenced. Third, we shall look at the way in which self-conception affects our goals in life and find that what we think of ourselves has much to do with our major aspirations as well as the effort we expend to reach our goals. We shall then turn to the dramatic aspect of self-conception, exploring the masks of identity used by people to achieve success. Finally, we shall deal with the pressing problem of self-alienation in contemporary society.

SOCIAL ATTRACTION AND THE SELF

Persons may love or hate each other for a variety of reasons, but fundamental to the feelings we have for others are the feelings we have for ourselves. Depending on our self-esteem we may be predisposed not only to feel certain ways about others in general, but also to respond favorably or unfavorably to their actions toward us. Let us take a closer look at each of these dispositions.

65

Self-Esteem and the Acceptance of Others

The noted psychoanalyst Erich Fromm was one of the first to observe the close connection between a person's evaluations of self and his feelings for others (1939). For Fromm, "Hatred against oneself is inseparable from hatred against others." On the basis of this observation, he considered low self-esteem, or excessive feelings of humility, to be a form of neurosis. Years later, Carl Rogers (1959) noted a similar phenomenon in many of his patients. Those who felt least capable of reaching their goals found it hardest to accept people around them.

There have subsequently been numerous attempts to document these observations more precisely. This research has been almost entirely correlational in nature, and almost without exception the results lend support to the earlier observations. Most typically, subjects or patients rate themselves on various tests of self-esteem and also evaluate other persons with whom they are acquainted. Positive correlations usually result, persons with high self-esteem showing greater acceptance of others.

Unfortunately, however, it is difficult to assess the significance of these results. Research on psychological assessment shows that people vary in their styles of filling out questionnaires or answering questions. For instance, some use extreme ends of scales while others tend to prefer more moderate answers. On tests of self-esteem and in rating other persons, extreme scorers tend to rate both themselves and others more positively (extremely negative scores are rare). Thus, positive correlations between self and other ratings could result from these stylistic modes of test-taking and have nothing to do with self-esteem per se. It seems, then, that although most of the available evidence corroborates the earlier observations, the crucial experiment remains to be done.

If self-esteem and esteem for others are indeed correlated, as the evidence suggests, we must ask why this should be so. Fromm has suggested that both feelings for self and feelings for others are based on the same set of childhood learning experiences. When children have been treated hostilely and their freedom has been spitefully curtailed, they develop a "character conditioned hatred" toward both self and others. Unfortunately, Fromm does not complete his argument by specifying exactly why this disposition should include both self and others. However, our analysis in Parts II and III does supply missing links. If a child has received continuous hostility from his parents and peers, a negative reaction to himself is quite likely to result from reflected appraisal. At the same time that he learns to dislike himself, he develops hatred for his parents and/or his peers. His subsequent dislike for other people may constitute a generalization from earlier experiences. On a subjective level the feeling might be, "I have always been treated badly, so what reason is there to suspect that others will be different?"

Rogers (1959) explains the relationship between self-esteem and acceptance of others in a slightly different way. For Rogers the regard received from others may be of two types: *conditional* or *unconditional*. Conditional regard is dependent on one's meeting the other's criteria of evaluation in order to be accepted; failure to meet his criteria leads to rejection. In contrast, unconditional regard is not dependent on the other's criteria of the evaluation. One is prized not for what he does but for his intrinsic value as a human being. Rogers observes that when regard is conditional, the person begins to evaluate himself conditionally—finding himself acceptable only if he meets certain criteria. When self-evaluation is conditional, the person defends against seeing himself in certain ways. He may distort his perception of self, avoid noticing certain of his actions, and, most important, be more defensive in social relationships. Since others may "show him up for what he is," he may avoid close contact or discredit their views. In effect, others are viewed as threats. Rogers, logically, is much opposed to the use of conditional regard in human relationships.

Another explanation of the relationship between regard for self and regard for others is that the person who feels inferior may not wish to admit to himself that others have positive attributes. To acknowledge others' superiority is to suffer through social comparison; to see them as inferior is to boost one's self-esteem. Through biased scanning one can always find shortcomings in others and in this way show himself that he is really not so bad after all.

Finally, there is a generalized tendency, when we have little clear information about another person, to assume that he is like ourselves (see Gergen, in press). If we feel afraid when walking on a darkened street, we assume that this is probably normal and that most others would feel the same way. Similarly, the person low in self-esteem may make certain assumptions about others' "true characteristics," assumptions that differ from those made by the person with high self-esteem. Which of these various factors produce the generally observed relationship between self-love and love for others and to what degree each is influential are questions for future research. Let us turn now to an aspect of attraction that has been more extensively studied.

Reactions to Others' Evaluations of Self

Feelings toward self may not only influence our generalized feelings toward others, but may also predispose us to react in specific ways to their behavior and evaluations of us. Typically, people tend to be attracted to those who evaluate them positively and to dislike those who appraise them negatively. There is considerable research to support this proposition; one example is a study by Jones, Gergen, and Davis (1962) in which undergraduate males were interviewed by advanced graduate students. After the interview half of the subjects learned that the graduate interviewer had a very positive opinion of them, while the other half learned that he disapproved of many of their personal characteristics. Subjects then evaluated the interviewer on a variety of dimensions. The results were clear: those receiving positive appraisals were overwhelmingly more positive in their evaluations of the interviewer.

In terms of self-theory, the reason for such results has been implicit in much that has been said thus far. We have seen, for example, that people are apt to incorporate positive facts about themselves more readily than negative facts, that they may accumulate goods in order to perceive themselves as superior to others, and that they tend to identify more completely with their roles when they receive positive reactions from others. All these observations point to the fact that self-esteem is all-important to the individual. Events or persons boosting one's esteem are gratifying and those which reduce it are abhorred. Rogers (1959) has spoken of a "basic need for self regard," a need that leads one to seek the regard of others. He has noted that in some clinical cases seeking the esteem of others seems more powerful a motive than physiological needs.

There is good reason to suspect that one's need for self-esteem develops in childhood. Essentially, it seems to depend on the close and frequent association between the reduction of physiological needs and feelings of being valuable. At the same time that a child is being fed he is also receiving the secondary message that he is valued. He may be fondled and caressed as an infant and may receive warm looks and affectionate talk as he grows older. He may be tickled when the wet, cold diaper is removed from his body and patted when a blanket is put over him to keep him warm. More subtly, by the very act of alleviating physical discomfort or increasing bodily pleasure, the other communicates to the child that he is esteemed.

The feeling of being valued or esteemed may be intrinsically neutral in tone. However, because of its frequent and continuous association with physical drive reduction, tactile pleasure, and the reduction of pain, it comes to have a learned value. An animal will seek out a chamber in which it has been fed long after the reward of food is no longer available, or it will expend great effort to escape a chamber in which it has been shocked long after the shock has been terminated. The animal acquires the motivation for stimuli that have been associated with basic states of pleasure or pain. In the same way, human feelings of being valuable have been associated with more basic states of pleasure and feelings of being valueless with states of pain or discomfort. As a result, the person learns to seek out the feeling of being esteemed for its own sake and to avoid the feeling of being valueless. To feel esteem for self is akin to one's most basic experience of well-being—the childhood experiences of being supported and nurtured by a benevolent environment. To be without esteem is symbolic of one's basic anguish in an unpredictable and uncontrollable world.

It follows from our discussion thus far that the more positive the appraisal we receive from another, the greater our attraction for him. However, let us turn to a study by Deutsch and Solomon (1959) and see how well this proposition holds up. In this experiment subjects worked together in groups to complete a difficult task. At a certain point in the procedure, each subject was given information indicating how much he had helped or hindered the group in reaching their goal. At random, half the subjects received information indicating that theirs had been one of the most outstanding contributions (success condition), while the other half learned that they had turned in the poorest performance in the group (failure condition). Although each subject received this information privately, he was led to believe that the others also knew of his rating. This manipulation was designed to create two groups, one with a temporary feeling of enhanced self-esteem and the other with a diminished regard for self.

Each subject then received a written evaluation from one of the other team members. By design, half the subjects in each of the above conditions received a positive evaluation. The fictitious team member praised them and said that he would be glad to have them on the team again (positive appraisal condition). The other half of the subjects received negative appraisals, wherein the team member criticized their performance and said that he would not like to have them continue on the team. All subjects then made a series of attraction ratings of the team member from whom they had received the appraisal. The major interest of the experiment was how attraction was affected by acceptance or rejection in states of high of low esteem.

Mean attraction scores for each of the four conditions appear in Table IV-1. Subjects who have succeeded (high self-esteem) react much as we have discussed. They are much more attracted to the person who appraises them positively than they are to a critic. But upon closer examination of the results we see another effect not previously accounted for. When subjects have failed (low self-esteem), they are more attracted to the critic than to the admirer. How can we account for this curious finding?

Table IV-1   Mean Attraction to Other Under Varying Conditions of Appraisal

| | | Other's Appraisal | |
		Positive	Negative
Subject Receives	Success	$\overline{X} = 8.6$	$\overline{X} = 7.7$
	Failure	$\overline{X} = 6.5$	$\overline{X} = 7.7$

NOTE: Data from 112 female telephone employees. Table adapted from Deutsch and Solomon, 1959. Original mean scores converted for clarity of presentation.

The one central feature of the condition in which low-esteem subjects are criticized is that the appraiser has been accurate in his judgment. When subjects fail and are praised, the appraiser has been grossly inaccurate in his estimates. It may be said, then, that *evaluation accuracy* plays an important role in our feelings toward someone who has appraised us. We may appreciate an accurate evaluator for several reasons. For one thing, he typically gives us information about ourselves that we can utilize. If we feel he is inaccurate in his estimates of us, he is irrelevant to our concern with developing a realistic and useful picture of self. Secondly, the credibility of the appraiser suffers when he is inaccurate. The inaccurate appraiser seems untrustworthy and possibly stupid. In addition, we are more likely to see the inaccurate appraiser as lacking in personalism. He may seem less attuned to us as persons and possibly influenced by ulterior motives. For a male to tell a female she is "beautiful" when she is feeling particularly unattractive may raise considerable suspicion about his motives. Additional research by Backman and Secord (1962) further highlights the importance of accuracy. In a study of friendship in a sorority, they found that girls preferred to do things with others who most agreed with their appraisals of themselves.

But we have yet to deal with the major paradox. What do we feel toward a person who evaluates us much more positively than we typically evaluate ourselves? On the one hand, the more positive the other's evaluation, the more gratifying to our needs for esteem. On the other hand, the greater the difference between self-evaluation and the other's evaluation of self, the less the perceived accuracy. In effect, these two processes tend to work against each other. The one predicts greater attraction as the other's evaluation becomes more positive (an esteem-enhancement effect), while the other predicts less attraction (an accuracy effect). Are we destined to accept the flatterer or sychophant who feeds our needs for esteem? Or must we forsake personal happiness in order to reject false praise? How is this conflict resolved?

It seems wise not to search for a universal answer to this question, that is, for a solution holding under all conditions. Rather, the specific conditions of a relationship may be all important. Certain conditions or factors may cause self-enhancement effects to predominate; other conditions may cause accuracy effects to hold sway. Five factors may be particularly important.

Characteristics of the evaluator   As we pointed out, part of the reason for disliking an inaccurate evaluator is that his inaccuracy reflects on his character. In particular, he may seem "stupid," "impersonal," or "driven by ulterior motives." It thus follows that any factors reinforcing such characterizations should enhance accuracy effects (reducing attraction) and offset the positive effects of esteem gratification.

An experiment by Dickoff (1961) nicely demonstrates this point. Undergraduate women participated in an interview procedure in which they were to be evaluated by a graduate student. One group of subjects found that the graduate student-evaluator (an experimental accomplice) agreed with their own evaluations of self very closely, while a second group found that the evaluator's appraisals of them were considerably more positive than their own self-ratings. Half the subjects in each of these groups were further told that it was the evaluator's task to be as honest as possible in her appraisals. The remaining half, however, were told that the graduate student wanted them to volunteer for an additional experiment—in other words, her motives for evaluating the subject were made to appear suspect. After the procedure subjects were asked to rate the evaluator. The results were clear: when the evaluator's motives seemed honest (that is, she could be trusted), subjects liked her much more when she had a high (but inflated) view of them. In contrast, when the evaluator's motives were suspect, there was no increase in attraction as she became more flattering. In fact, there was a tendency for her to be liked less when she was flattering than when her appraisals corresponded to the subjects' own self-estimates.

Characteristics of the evaluation: Conditional versus unconditional   Evaluations received from others vary in a number of ways. Of particular importance is the distinction between conditional versus unconditional appraisals. The folk-rock singer Bob Dylan once wrote a song in which he addressed a young lady with a long list of things he wasn't setting out to do. He was not there to "analyze her," "criticize her," or "make eyes at her." All he wished was to be her "friend." Dylan's song captures the essence of unconditional evaluations as contrasted to conditional evaluations. Conditional evaluations are tied to specific characteristics or behavior. As we explained earlier, the person is evaluated positively or liked because of specific things that he does or is capable of doing. By implication he would not be acceptable if he did not do these things. Grading systems consist of conditional evaluations and, unfortunately, so do many love or friendship relations. Unconditional approval is effusive and expresses generalized good-will, a positive feeling that exists without regard to the person's specific behavior. As in the Dylan song, the simple expression of friendship is unconditional; the positive feelings do not depend on a series of activities that the person might be called on to perform.

Both conditional and unconditional evaluations may enhance one's self-esteem. Receiving hugs and kisses after winning a race may be as gratifying as receiving an unsolicited expression of warmth. However, our orientations are not the same for both; we do not look to both for the same thing. With conditional evaluations, a higher premium is placed on accuracy. Such evaluations inform us that we have performed well or poorly and knowledge of the success of performance may be useful on future occasions. In matters of friendship, companionship, or love, however, unconditional evaluations are usually more relevant. Here we may not wish the other's evaluations to depend on our performance at the moment. In such instances, attraction to the other should increase as he is more positive toward us. Accuracy should be a minor concern.

Characteristics of the situation: The demand for accuracy   Certain situations place a strong premium on being accurate about oneself. It would be unprofitable to enter a beauty contest without others' honest evaluations of one's talents and appearance or to set out to save a drowning man without an accurate estimate of one's own ability to swim. When rewards and punishments are contingent on accuracy, the person should be less attracted to inaccurate appraisals from others. As Pepitone (1967) has suggested, this set toward accuracy may account for the Deutsch and Soloman results discussed above. The task on which subjects were caused to succeed or fail involved their abilities to form accurate impressions. The situation emphasized the importance of being accurate; therefore, subjects may have been especially inclined to reject inaccurate appraisals of themselves by others.

The need for self-esteem   People clearly differ in the extent to which they fulfill their need for self-esteem. Although social approval is readily available to some persons, others may be chronically impoverished. Success or failure may also affect our esteem needs at any moment. If we fail, our esteem is temporarily lowered and our need is greater. When one's esteem needs are unfulfilled, the approval of others becomes particularly valuable. It is the person most deficient in self-esteem who most exerts himself to obtain it. Most touching is the individual so lacking the love or affection of others that his grasping demands stifle precisely those who might be able to fulfill his needs.

One's need for self-esteem has a direct bearing on his reaction to others' evaluations. The person who is deprived of support, either chronically or at one particular time, should be most gratified by a positive evaluation. For him, evaluation accuracy should have little importance. When his esteem is high, he should be less attracted to one who evaluates him positively and unrealistically.

Support for this position is found in an engaging study carried out by Walster (1965). In this experiment Stanford coeds filled out a battery of personality questionnaires. While each subject waited for the next phase of the experiment, a handsome male student (an experimental accomplice) "happened in." He struck up a conversation and after 15 minutes asked the subject out for a date. After he left, the experimenter gave the subject an evaluation of certain aspects of her personality. At random, half the subjects were told they were deficient in a number of respects (for example, immature)—in effect, their need for self-esteem was temporarily increased. The other half were told they were vastly superior to others taking the same tests. Their esteem needs were presumably lowered as a result. As part of a separate study the subject was then asked to evaluate her parents, friends, and, most important, the male visitor.

Attraction to the flattering male differed significantly for subjects in the two conditions. Those who had experienced a temporary deficit in self-esteem reacted much more positively; failure on the test made them more vulnerable to the male's attention. Those who had been praised were quite neutral in their feelings about him. To lack self-regard causes one to be much more appreciative of regard from others, whether they are sincere or not.[1]

Functional value of relevant concepts   As we saw in Part II, concepts differ in their functional value to the person. Holding the concept of himself as "intelligent" may render a person less vulnerable to others' attacks and allow him to engage in social relations without anxiety. Other concepts, such as "great grandson" may be less generally important; these are used

---

[1] This argument is further expanded in Berscheid and Walster (1969), pp. 60–61.

less often in achieving goals. It seems quite likely that for concepts of great functional value, self-enhancement is preeminent. When it is important for a person to see himself in a certain way, receiving strong support (even if inaccurate) for this self-view may well yield attraction. On the other hand, if the aspect of self has little value to the person, praise is less gratifying and accuracy considerations may have greater weight. This reasoning leads to the conclusion that the more important a particular self-view is to the person, the more susceptible he is to the inflated and flattering remarks of others. But empirical evidence to support this is needed.

To summarize, positive evaluations from others often produce conflict. Because such evaluations boost esteem, we may be attracted to the evaluator. But to the extent that these same evaluations exceed our current estimate of self, they also seem inaccurate and the evaluator is then disliked. The relative strength of these opposing tendencies will depend on a variety of factors. Factors reducing the evaluator's credibility or personalism will reduce attraction. When conditional evaluations are at stake, accuracy will be more valued than when unconditional evaluations are desired. If the situation is one in which rewards are contingent on being accurate about self, accuracy effects will dominate. Persons whose need for esteem is great will also be more appreciative of another's positive evaluation. Finally, the greater the functional value of a particular self-view to the person, the greater his appreciation of positive appraisal.

POWER, INFLUENCE, AND THE SELF

People vary greatly in their capacity to influence or control the behavior of those about them. In large organizations such as industry or government, one's power is largely determined by his formal position within the hierarchy. In most interpersonal relationships, however, the extent to which one individual determines the destiny of his associates is highly reliant on his personal characteristics. What type of person, by virtue of training or basic temperament, will be motivated to influence others? What type of person is more apt to be influenced? Although such questions cannot be answered simply, we can begin by considering *self-conception*.

First, how is it that some persons have such great influence over their peers? Many studies suggest that an individual's esteem for himself is strongly related to the amount of pressure he exerts on others. In an early study by Thomas and Burdick (1954), individuals with generally high esteem, as indicated on a self-assessment measure, were paired together and asked to reach a joint conclusion in diagnosing several case histories. Other two-man groups were composed of persons low in self-esteem. In ratings made after the discussions, members of high-esteem groups rated each other as attempting to influence them more often than members of low-esteem groups did. Cohen (1956) reached similar conclusions, and also found that high self-esteem persons rated themselves higher in attempted influence as well.

The fascinating work of Hastorf, Bavelas, Gross, and Kite (see Hastorf, 1970) is also relevant to the point at hand. Subjects participated in discussions in groups of six persons. Before each subject was placed a signal light that only he could see. The signal was controlled by trained observers behind a one-way mirror, and it indicated to the subject when he should feel free to speak and when he should refrain from doing so. During the first part of this research, subjects were all given a "go" signal for 15 minutes. During this period it could be determined which subject was quietest or least motivated to lead the group discussion. Then, all subjects were signalled to refrain from speaking except this one. The result was dramatic. During the next 15 minutes signs of timidity began to vanish, and the chosen individual came to dominate the group discussion. During a third 15-minute segment, all participants were again given the "go" signal. The esteem-boosting effects of speaking out while the others attentively listened seemed to have lasting effects on the speaker. Not only did the originally timid member become one of the group's most dominant contributors, but team members later rated him as one of the most influential members of the group. High self-esteem, then, seems strongly related to an individual's social power.

Many studies demonstrate that low self-esteem is closely related to one's tendency to accept the influence attempts of others. Although most of this research has been conducted with adolescent or adult samples, a study by Lesser and Abelson (1959) is especially interesting because it suggests that susceptibility to influence may be learned at an early age. Grammar school children were first tested for generalized self-esteem in an ingenious manner. Each child was shown a large card on which appeared photographs of each of his classmates. His first task was to compare himself with other children in the class on a series of characteristics. He was asked, for example, to indicate all the children in the class who were "nicer" than he, "smarter," "more polite," and so on. The child's self-esteem score was determined by the number of children he did not judge superior to himself; when few children were judged superior, the child was said to have high self-esteem. A second measure was derived from the child's responses when asked which children in the class "liked him" or "would like to sit next to him." The greater the number of children named by the subject, the higher his self-esteem score. For this study, scores for these two measures were combined and children were divided into two groups, those with low and those with high self-esteem.

In order to test the extent to which each group would yield to social influence, the experimenter presented 14 pairs of pictures to each of the 56 subjects. The experimenter indicated which of the two pictures she preferred (predetermined on a random basis) and then asked the subject to name a preference. The amount of influence was measured by the number of times the subject agreed with the experimenter. For those whose self-esteem was low, the mean number of agreements with the experimenter was over twelve. In contrast, high self-esteem children agreed with the experimenter on the average of only eight out of fourteen trials, barely exceeding chance.[2]

We have now seen that there is strong support for the proposition that high self-esteem persons tend to be more powerful in social relationships; they attempt more to influence others and they are less susceptible to others' attempts to influence them. As yet, however, research has not answered the question of precisely why this is so. A number of factors may be determinant. First, we have already seen that low-esteem persons are generally more anxious to have others' acceptance and support. Attempts to influence others involves a great risk of alienating them and might thus be avoided by this group, while accepting others' opinions and yielding to their desires may often gain their acceptance. Second, low-esteem persons may be less confident in their opinions and judgments. Typically, such persons have not benefitted from the praise of others and may feel unsure about the validity of their views. They should thus be reticent in drawing others to their position and more accepting of what they feel to be authoritative opinions.

Cohen (1959) has also argued that high and low esteem is accompanied by different psychological defenses. When a person is high in esteem and satisfied with himself and his world-view, he may wish to remain invulnerable. He therefore tries to bring others to his position and to avoid whatever might threaten him with change. In contrast, the low-esteem individual has little to lose by change and may even long to be

---

[2] It should be further noted that this effect was most striking when preliminary experience with the experimenter had been positive. That is, when the experimenter's praise was available the low self-esteem children were most conforming. When her approval was not available, high and low-esteem children differed little in their conformity. This finding is especially pertinent to understanding the dynamics underlying the relationship between self-esteem and persuasibility.

remolded for the better. From this viewpoint, the incessant joiner of social groups, or "true believer" as Eric Hoffer has labelled him, may be one who is not so much dissatisfied with the state of the world as he is with himself. But again, further research will be needed to clarify many of these issues.[3] We may now turn to a third way in which self-conception affects our behavior.

SELF-CONCEPTION AND PERSONAL ASPIRATIONS

We have already seen that aspirations may bias self-conception. Wanting to be something can influence one to see himself as he wishes to be. Yet, one's conception of self can also affect his aspirations—what he chooses to do and how much effort he expends in doing it. The primary reason is that people aspire to do that which will yield success and shun activities which may lead to failure. Self-conception is central to this process in two ways.

The first is implicit in our earlier discussions of esteem needs. "Success" in the above formulation usually involves gaining social approval, either real or implied, and thus feeling enhanced esteem for self. Being a college president is one of the most taxing occupations available to men of high calibre. Those who fill such positions could amass greater wealth, have greater freedom, and be less nettled in dozens of other positions. However, the position can be highly gratifying to one's self-esteem. The prestige of being "president," the belief that one is furthering the aims of education, and a unique position in one's community all lead to this end.

Second, in order to gauge the probability of succeeding at a given activity we must have some idea of our own capacities. Whether we play bridge with experts depends on how we appraise our sophistication at the game, and whether we choose to attend college depends in part on how we estimate our mental capacities. Our aspirations thus depend on our estimates of self.

Let us examine data from two studies related to these arguments. In the first, Backman and Secord (1968) studied the preferences of undergraduate females for certain marital roles. Earlier research had isolated three major types of roles: the traditional *wife-and-mother role,* in which

---

[3] These arguments must be qualified in one important way. Almost all the research reporting a positive relationship between self-esteem and persuasibility has used male subjects; the relationship between the two variables may be different for females. Both Cox and Bauer (1964) and Gergen and Bauer (1967) have found that low self-esteem females reject influence attempts in the same way that high-esteem females do. With women, medium-esteem females seem to be most conforming.

the woman is expected to bear and rear children, care for the home, and maintain a dependent economic and social status; the *companion role,* in which she shares a variety of pleasures and activities with her husband, strives to be attractive, intellectually challenging, and stimulating, and cultivates social contacts; and the *partner role,* in which she has equal authority in making family decisions, maintains an independent career and does not provide domestic services. These roles were described in greater detail to the students, and they were asked to order their preference for each. On a separate occasion they were asked to judge themselves in relation to a variety of traits such as "absent-minded," "ambitious," "bossy," and "cautious." A group of independent raters then judged each of the role models on the same series of traits. (For example, the partner role might be rated high on "ambition" while the wife-and-mother role would receive a low rating on this trait.)

Armed with these data the investigators asked whether the students' judgments of self would predict their preferences for roles as adults. The answer to this question was highly affirmative. The findings showed that the closer the subject's self-descriptions were to the characteristics of a given role, the greater the preference for the role. Students seeing themselves as "ambitious," then, would prefer the role of partner to the role of wife-and-mother, while girls rating themselves as "cautious" were less likely to prefer the partner role.

Although this research documents the close relationship between self-conception and aspirations for the future, it does not demonstrate that self-conception affects actual behavior. Can we move from the level of what one plans to do to what he actually does? A laboratory experiment by Diggory, Klein, and Cohen (1964) not only shows the close tie between self-conception and behavior but, in addition, highlights the close dependency of this process on the individual's momentary experience of success and failure. In this experiment, naval personnel worked on a difficult symbol-sorting task. Each subject was exposed to a series of cards, on each of which was printed one of ten different symbols. For each symbol there was a corresponding number displayed nearby. When a symbol card was presented it was the subject's task to look up or try to remember the corresponding number and to tap out this number on a telegraph key placed by his right hand. There were to be ten one-minute trials, and it was the subject's task to reach a performance level of 40 correct responses per trial.

Since the experimenter was in a position to announce the subject's score at the end of each trial, he could also control his success and failure at will. All subjects were informed that they were continually improving.

However, as the trials progressed, half the subjects (success condition) found that if their rate of improvement continued they might reach the desired criterion. The other half (failure condition) saw that their rate of improvement could not possibly yield success.

The dependent variables in the study were two in number: first, the subject's written estimate after every trial of the probability that he could finally succeed (a self-estimate of capability); and second, a measure of muscle tension or work performance. The latter measure was obtained by attaching electrodes to the right arm of the subject and recording electrically the moment-to-moment state of the muscles. Two measures of muscular activity were obtained: the state of the muscles while actually performing the task and muscle tension when the subject was at rest or waiting to perform the task.

In Figure IV-1 are plotted the results for these various measures.

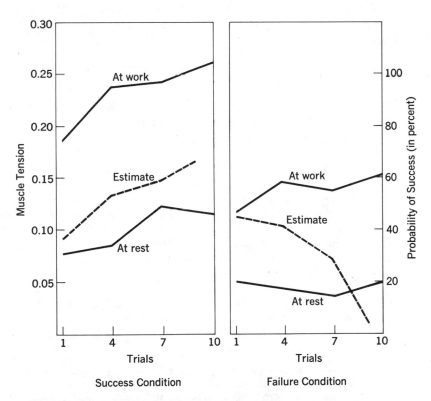

Success Condition   Failure Condition

Figure IV-1
Probability of Success and Muscle Tension as a Function of Task Success versus Failure.

We can first examine the subjects' estimates of whether they felt they could succeed. As might be expected, the difference between these ratings in the success as opposed to the failure condition is dramatic. In the former, subjects increasingly feel they are capable of succeeding, while in the latter there is a continuous drop in these estimates. Estimates of one's capacities is highly dependent, then, on the moment-to-moment feedback provided by the environment. But what happens to actual performance of work? As we can see, muscle activity is also affected as the subject sees himself more or less capable of achieving his goal. Not only under working conditions do the success subjects show greater muscle tension, but also under conditions of rest. In essence, they remain tense and involved when they feel they are capable of succeeding. When it appears they will fail, subjects diminish their effort.[4] Not to believe that you are capable of success may actually guarantee your failure.

Having seen how self-conception is related to social attraction, power, and aspirations, we are in a position to consider the problem of self-presentation.

THE PRESENTATION OF SELF

We are indebted to Erving Goffman for directing attention to the following account of Preedy, an Englishman who is making his first appearance on the beach at a summer vacation spot:

> But in any case he took care to avoid catching anyone's eye. First of all, he had to make it clear to those potential companions of his holiday that they were of no concern to him whatsoever. He stared through them, round them, over them—eyes lost in space. The beach might have been empty. If by chance a ball was thrown his way, he looked surprised; then let a smile of amusement lighten his face (Kindly Preedy), looked around dazed to see that there *were* people on the beach, tossed it back with a smile to himself and not a smile at the people, and then resumed carelessly his nonchalant survey of space.
>
> But it was time to institute a little parade, the parade of the Ideal Preedy. By devious handlings he gave any who wanted a chance to see the title of his book—a Spanish translation of Homer, classic thus, but not

---

[4] A delightful study by Kiesler and Baral (1970) extends the implications of this finding. These investigators found that male college students whose self-esteem was temporarily increased were more likely to seek out an attractive girl for a date than an unattractive one. In contrast, if self-esteem was temporarily lowered, their aspirations were lowered and an unattractive girl was more likely to be approached than an attractive one.

daring, cosmopolitan too—and then gathered together his beach-wrap and bag into a neat sand-resistant pile (Methodical and Sensible Preedy), rose slowly to stretch his huge frame (Big-Cat Preedy), and tossed aside his sandals (Carefree Preedy, after all) [Sansom, 1956, pp. 230–231].

Undoubtedly, all of us can recognize a bit of Preedy in ourselves, as distasteful as the image may be. But we are all faced with the important task of providing others with an idea of who we are, for until others can identify us they cannot know how to behave toward us. To be a "foreigner" or "mentally ill," for instance, is of crucial significance for others in determining their actions. By the same token, the definition we present to others influences our level of reward or punishment in the relationship. To present oneself as "gruff" and "ill-tempered" is usually to reduce the pleasure we receive at the hands of others. Finally, by defining ourselves to others we can better predict their behavior. We know that to be perceived as "rich" yields certain responses; to be seen as "poor" yields different ones. Through self-presentation, the environment moves from a random state to one of order.

Self-conception has obvious implications for the way we publicly present ourselves to others. It would be very handy, of course, if there were a one-to-one relationship between people's private and public definitions of self. We could then be sure of the other's behavior and where we stood with respect to him. Indeed, Western culture generally condemns those whose public face differs from their private conception of self. We find this view reflected in Shakespeare's "To thine own self be true" as well as the contemporary country and western refrain:

> I'm just a country boy
> But there's one thing sure as shootin'
> I can't stand those folks who think
> They're so dad-burn high fallutin'
> I'd be the same in Hollywood
> As right in my own kitchen
> I believe in fussin' when you're mad
> And scratchin' when you're itchin'.

However, it is probable that this felicitous state does not commonly exist. A wide number of factors cause the person to shift his public identity as an actor in ancient times might have changed masks from one scene to the next.

What are the primary factors that produce such chameleon-like activity? Essentially, the major sources of influence fall into three main categories: the *other,* the *interaction environment,* and *motivation.* We shall briefly discuss each in turn.

The Other

The identity of the other person and his behavior toward us can be central in determining the self-image that we present. If you have ever moved rapidly from one group to another or from one friend to another, you have undoubtedly noticed this fact in yourself. You may be energetic and happy-go-lucky with friends but appear serious and conscientious when conferring with a banker, and the "ideal" characteristics of self you present in a romantic relationship may jar with your identity as viewed by a brother or sister. As William James has said, a man has "as many different social selves as there are distinct groups of persons about whose opinion he cares" (1892).

Those around us may affect our "social selves" in three ways, two of which are familiar to us. First, others are continuously teaching us who we are. Others have varying images of us and depending on these images they treat us as a particular kind of person. Weinstein (1967) has called this process *altercasting.* We are cast into specific roles or identities by those around us. At the same time we are being cast into a particular identity, each of us harbors a multitude of self-concepts in various stages of development. Thus, the cues that others give to us about ourselves serve to reinforce certain of these concepts and reduce the salience of others. Continuous learning about self thus takes place.

A second reason that we shift public identities is related to the first. As pointed out earlier, we develop over time certain ways of viewing ourselves in the presence of particular people. With Fred we may have learned to see ourselves as "intense" and "philosophical," whereas Susan has always made us realize that we are "superficially frivolous." According to principles of association learning, the sheer presence of these persons should thereafter serve to elicit these differential views of self. We react with the "self" learned in the presence of the other. To spot Susan on the street may cause our face to blossom in smile, while our reaction to Fred's appearance may be an anguished grimace and eyes turned upwards toward the heavens.

Of course, both of these processes are "honest" ones; that is, the person may be fully convinced of the accuracy of his overt presentation at the moment. A third process, however, borders on a more selfish side of everyday relations. We are all interested in maximizing our benefits in social relations. We seek rewards and do our best to avoid punishment.

The characteristics of others and their behavior toward us serve as cues for effective maximization. They aid us in performing optimally, often without regard to our sincerity.

While Goffman (1959, 1961) has discussed numerous ways in which this maximization takes place, an experiment by Gergen and Wishnov (1965) presents empirical evidence. The special interest of the study was in people's reactions to others who differ in self-esteem—from the flamboyant egotist to the diffident "poor mouth." It was reasoned that people who are extreme in their self-praise or their self-condemnation raise particular tactical problems for those who interact with them.

The egotist creates a power problem. By accentuating his virtues he implies that others are not equal to him. His manner bespeaks his assumption that he deserves status, a greater share of whatever rewards are available, and the right to lead in decision making. Skillful self-presentation may be helpful in dealing with this kind of person; in particular, we might well react in kind, accentuating our assets and hiding our shortcomings. The self-derogator presents a far different type of problem. We may wish to nurture or aid him out of commiseration and at the same time wish to avoid further dealings with him because he seems so weak and dependent. Thus, we might be inclined to admit that we have shortcomings but not wish to identify ourselves as being on the same level as the other.

As a means of observing such strategies in action, undergraduate females were asked during a class period to rate themselves on a series of positive and negative characteristics (for example, "I am generally attractive to others," "I am often nervous and anxious"). Approximately one month later they participated in an experiment in which they were to exchange a set of written communications with another coed whose identity was unknown to them. These communications would "allow them to get acquainted" more rapidly. During this exchange, each subject received a set of self-ratings supposedly filled out by her partner. By design, one group received a set of ratings in which the partner described herself in most glowing terms. She enjoyed her work, her dating life, her home and saw herself as having no faults, but many virtues (egotism condition). A second experimental group received a self-description from the supposed partner that was quite opposite in character. She felt distinct lacks in all aspects of her life and saw numerous faults in herself with no redeeming virtues (humility condition). It was then the subject's turn to respond, and in part this response took the form of self-ratings of the same variety she had made a month earlier. The major interest of the study was to see the way she would change these ratings in reaction to the partner's rating.

Self-rating change on both positive and negative characteristics is found in Figure IV-2. Both egotism and humility have strikingly different effects on the way subjects identify themselves. The egotist causes them to become much more positive about themselves—boosting their positive characteristics and de-emphasizing their negative ones—in an apparent attempt to offset the power balance. Humility, in contrast, causes subjects to portray themselves as being much more fault-ridden in terms of their characterizations on negative traits. However, they are not willing to give up their claim to positive qualities. When faced with another's humiliation, the reaction seems to be one of commiserating by showing faults but retaining independence through the maintenance of positive characteristics.

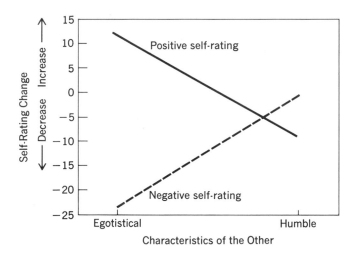

Figure IV-2
Self-Rating Change Produced by an Egotistical versus a Humble Other.

The Interaction Environment

In determining the self that we present, the environment in which the encounter takes place is as important as others' identities. We are not likely to identify ourselves in the same way at a formal dance as we do in a pool hall, regardless of who is present. Situations bring about shifts in identity primarily because they offer cues for maximization of reward. For example, we know from past experience what patterns of behavior are expected in varying circumstances. We know that we are expected to be polite and reserved in a religious setting, and, therefore, to avoid censure we may create the impression (however mistaken) of being a "perfect gentleman." Likewise, immediate situations themselves have ways of creating exigent behaviors. In team sports, cooperation is the keynote, in debating, rationality and rhetoric are necessary to achieve success. As Goffman (1961) has shown, even patients entering a mental institution must learn how to behave as "proper" psychotics.

Environmental cues are demonstrated in a study by Gergen and Taylor (1969). Junior and senior ROTC students were to work together in pairs on one of two types of tasks. Half the subject pairs were to work on a task that demanded great productivity—maneuvering a mock submarine out of danger in a complex situation. The other half of the subjects were given a task for which social compatibility was most important—being understanding and tolerant in working out a set of ship maneuvers. Before work began each subject was to describe himself to his partner (who was either higher or lower than himself in ROTC rank) in order that they could be "better acquainted." The results showed that regardless of rank subjects in the productivity setting became more positive about themselves. They represented themselves as having many more positive qualities than they had professed a month earlier on a similar measure. Exactly the reverse took place when compatibility was at stake. In an apparent attempt to make themselves seem more "human" and less defensive, subjects de-emphasized their virtues and were more willing to admit shortcomings. On the job, people seem bent on displaying virtues; in social settings they are more likely to underestimate themselves.

Personal Motivation

The individual's presentation of self may be determined also by his motives in a relationship. If a person wishes to be treated with deference, his demeanor may be marked by superiority; if he wishes to be trusted, he may insure that his behavior is always consistent. Research on the effects of motivation on self-presentation has primarily concentrated on approval seeking. How do people manage their public identity in order to acquire the liking and acceptance of others? Unsurprisingly, the results of such studies (see Jones, Gergen, & Davis, 1962) show that in order to gain approval people typically emphasize their positive characteristics and withhold their personal failings from public view.

One exception to the general rule has been found (Jones, Gergen, & Jones, 1963). In this study it was discovered that in order to gain favor among their subordinates senior members of an organization presented themselves less positively on characteristics that were not relevant to their position of command. As Blau (1964) has reasoned, the senior person is seen by his juniors as remote, aloof, and threatening. By suggesting that he, too, has shortcomings, the senior member makes himself more accessible. Of course, he does it in such a way as not to undermine his position of seniority—the boss may admit he is a terrible golfer to facilitate interaction, but he is much less likely to admit that he sometimes makes poor professional decisions.

This discussion of self-presentation has emphasized the fact that people will often forego their true conceptions of self for purposes of social gain. However, before responding indignantly to the charade that surrounds us, we must take note of people's experience as they play the game. In a number of studies just discussed, subjects have been asked about their experiences—how honest did they feel they could be, how sincere did they feel, to what extent did the other person or situation make a difference to their behavior, and so forth. Responses to such questions typically reveal that people do *not* generally feel insincere when they alter their social identity. They may describe themselves in one way at one moment and the reverse the next, and feel equally honest and sincere at both times. This finding is quite consistent with our earlier discussions of self-concept learning and role playing. As we pointed out, a person may harbor a variety of concepts of himself which differ in salience from moment to moment. When a particular role is used in a particular situation, the salience of certain concepts may increase and others may be lost from awareness. Thus, self-presentation may convince a person for the moment that he is indeed what he says he is. To be sure, not all presentation is accompanied by feelings of "true self." Highly learned concepts of self may be continuously salient and nag one when he violates them. However, there is a strong tendency in social relations for the person to become the mask.

THE PROBLEM OF SELF-ALIENATION

It has often been said that we are currently living in an age of alienation. Alienation is revealed in almost all aspects of cultural life. We see it in our theater with characters like Tennessee Williams' Mrs. Stone, who "pursued the little diversions, the hairdressers at four o'clock, the photographer at 5:00, the Colony at 6:00, the theater at 7:30, Sardi's at midnight . . . she moved in the great empty circle. But she glanced inward from the periphery and saw the void. . . ." Albert Camus' novel *The Stranger* stands as a classic portrayal of a man detached from self and others. In theology, we find the words of Kierkegaard: "By seeing the multitude of men about it, by getting engaged in all sorts of worldly affairs, by becoming wise about how things go in the world . . . a man forgets himself . . . does not dare to believe in himself, finds it too venturesome a thing to be himself, far easier and safer to be like others, to become an imitation, a number, a cipher in the crowd." If we turn to Jaspers' philosophical writings we find concern with "a loneliness of soul such as never existed before, a loneliness that hides itself, that seeks relief in vain in the erotic or the irrational until it leads eventually to a deep comprehension of the importance of establishing *communication* between man and man."

In the field of political theory, one of the most significant statements concerning alienation was made by Karl Marx in 1848. Marx felt that man's labor in a capitalistic system alienates him from himself. He contended that a worker functions as a pawn, forced by his poverty to carry out the will of others in producing objects that he cannot himself own. Because of this, he becomes alienated from his work; being alienated from his work, he is also alienated from himself. The endless hours spent in working do not reflect his spontaneous desires or his felt potential.

Psychiatric writings have also begun to reflect this concern with alienation. The noted analyst Karen Horney observed in many of her patients a "loss of feeling [self] as an organic whole . . . an alienation from the real self" (1950). Indeed it has been said that, "The main characteristic of today's patient is his estrangement from himself" (Weiss, 1961).

It is beyond the scope of this volume to deal with alienation in all its manifestations. However, if our earlier thinking about self-conception is valid, it should aid us in understanding one form of alienation, self-alienation. What lies beneath this feeling of disconnectedness? What are the processes at stake? And if this is an age of self-alienation, what social conditions give rise to this state?

First, how are we to understand the phenomenon of self-alienation? It is apparent from what we have said that the feeling is intensely unpleasant; symptoms such as anxiety, nausea, and depression may all be present. It is also clear that this negative feeling is not synonymous with low self-esteem. A person may feel quite at home with the notion that he is inferior. It seems more profitable, then, to view self-alienation as a *noxious feeling arising when overt actions are detached or inconsistent with underlying conceptions of self.* That is, self-alienation can be viewed as estrangement of the concept world from the daily activities of the individual. The individual might feel, "What I'm doing doesn't reveal the real me," "My behavior is a sham," or in its extreme form, "I hate what I do."

Starting from this point, we can ask in theoretical terms how a person comes to feel estranged from his behavior. It first seems apparent that all self-alienation is not the same, but may rather stem from a variety of sources. If we disentangle the threads of experience, we can identify three major sources of self-alienation.

The first source was implied in our earlier discussions of self-consistency and roles. As we saw, a person learns in varying degrees to seek and maintain consistency among his various conceptions of self. Inconsistency may produce the noxious state we have called dissonance. If a person's behavior appears inconsistent with his major ways of conceiving of himself, he may also have the negative experience of dissonance. Thus, a person who defines himself as a pacifist would feel self-alienated if he engaged in violent activities, whether by rioting or by carrying war into other nations; a self-defined conservative would feel self-alienated wearing mod clothes; and a student who saw himself as honest would be self-alienated if under pressure he were to cheat on an exam. In all cases the person is self-alienated because his behavior is inconsistent with his conception of himself.

A more powerful source of self-alienation stems from situations in which *behavior violates identity aspirations.* Here the person's behavior is inconsistent not so much with what he feels he is, but with what he wishes to become. A woman who strives to be respected for her opinions or contribution to society at large may often find herself stifled by maintaining a household; a Negro male who wishes to be esteemed by his family may become self-alienated when he must take a job that is degrading. Self-alienation is potentially more profound in such cases because it comes from two sources. First, there is the dissonance produced by the logical inconsistency between behavior and aspirations. And in addition to dissonance there is the accompanying frustration of being unable to fulfill aspirations. Every moment spent in cleaning house is a moment subtracted from becoming liberated; every hour on a self-demeaning job is an hour lost in seeking more fulfilling employment.

A third and more subtle source of self-alienation may be traced to instances in which *behavior is unrelated to the person's most salient ways of viewing himself.* Because the patterns of daily life are largely repetitive, a close relationship exists between a man's major conceptions of himself and his behavior. With repetitive behavior, labels become reinforced and people continuously teach the person a single identity. In such circumstances the individual becomes completely identified with his behavior. On the other hand, there are many instances in which a sudden shift in life situation wrenches our behavior from our major self-conceptions.

Going to college, marrying, taking a new job, and becoming a parent are only a few of these instances. In each, the person may initially feel estranged from his behavior. Not knowing precisely how to act, running the risk of failure in not knowing, feeling as if the actions are out of joint with standard modes of being—all contribute to feelings of estrangement. One of the most common forms of this type of alienation results from upward mobility in a society. When an individual increases his income, he often shifts neighborhoods, friends, possessions, work locale, and so on. Unfortunately, his self-conception is not so flexible. Thus, he finds himself overtly engaged in a new life but his identity continues to haunt him. A man who has lived most of his life in a rural setting moves to the city only to despise the "superficiality" of his life; the man eating caviar in a white tie may yearn for the simplicity of corn on the cob in the kitchen. There is additional evidence from the field of mental health showing that rapid upward mobility is significantly correlated with mental illness.

To understand the psychological sources of self-alienation is not to understand why the issue has become such a pervasive one within our culture. Is there reason to believe that self-alienation is more prevalent at this time in history than ever before? It appears so. If there is one major change that has taken place in the quality of social life it is its *increased multiplexity*—the number and variety of relationships in which we engage have steadily increased. This change is based on a number of factors. First, there are simply more people living in the same land area than ever before. As the economy has shifted from an agricultural to an industrial basis, the population has shifted from rural to metropolitan areas—that is, areas of greater population density. In addition, communication facilities have improved markedly. For example, people can be reached by telephone almost any time, at almost any place, from almost any part of the world. More rapid means of transportation make us additionally vulnerable to social impingements and at the same time enable us to encounter more people in less time. We are exposed to a host of others through modern mass communications facilities and people live out relationships with those encountered in the media, whether real or imaginary.

What does this increased multiplexity of social life have to do with self-alienation? With each new relationship, new behavioral demands are placed on the person; each new relationship requires a unique form of adaptation. Under these conditions the likelihood of engaging in behavior inconsistent with major ways of viewing self, behavior that violates identity aspirations, and behavior that is unrelated to major conceptions of self is maximal. When a wife, children, car-pool cronies, secretary, boss, subordinates, office messenger, colleagues of equal rank, business and personal acquaintances who visit or call, bartender, waiter, newsstand manager, barber, drop-in or back-fence neighbors, in-laws, Vladimir Nabokov, and Johnny Carson must all be catered to, grappled with, confronted, cajoled, influenced, loved, punished, taught, or escaped within one day, maintaining an integral sense of identity is a laborious task at best. In essence, multiplex demands and expectations constitute a generating milieu for self-alienation.

One peculiar paradox follows from this analysis. To be maximally adaptive in a multiplex social environment is to be maximally vulnerable to experiences of self-alienation. In order to relate successfully over a wide range of relationships, it is virtually impossible to bind our behavior to a limited set of self-conceptions. Self-alienation, then, may be viewed as a necessary by-product of successful adaptation in a complex social world. Whether self-alienation is worth the price is a matter of personal decision.

SUMMARY

In this final part we have discussed several major ways in which self-conception influences behavior. First we saw that negative feelings toward self may predispose one negatively toward others. We then asked how people respond emotionally to acceptance and rejection from others. In the main, we saw that because acceptance gratifies one's needs for self-esteem, it generates attraction. However, this general statement was complicated by the desire to have others provide accurate evaluations. The way people react when others evaluate them more positively than they evaluate themselves was seen to depend primarily on how one assesses the other's character, whether the evaluations are conditional or unconditional, situational demands for accuracy, the person's need for self-esteem, and the functional value of the concepts involved. We then turned to the question of power and influence. Here we found good evidence that persons low in self-esteem are less prone to influence others and more inclined to be influenced. In dealing with aspirations and life goals, we found that one's estimate of self strongly influences his goals and his behavior in reaching these goals. We then focussed on self-presentation behavior to find that our social identity is only partly determined by self-conception. Other influential factors include the characteristics and the behavior of others toward us, the environment at the moment, and our motivation. In our final discussion we dealt with three separate sources of self-alienation. Here we found that certain features of contemporary society tend to increase self-alienation. Throughout this discussion, we have seen that self-conception plays a critical role in the individual's private emotional life, as well as in his relationships with others. There is much we do not yet know about the formation and subsequent impact of self-conception. Future research in this area should indeed be rewarding.

REFERENCES

Allport, G. W. *Becoming.* New Haven, Conn.: Yale University Press, 1954 (On pp. 35 and following, one of the classic arguments in support of self-theory and against positivistic imperialism).

Backman, C. W., & Secord, P. F. Liking, selective interaction and misperception in congruent interpersonal relations. *Sociometry,* 1962, **25,** 321–335.

Backman, C. W., & Secord, P. F. The self and role selection. In C. Gordon & K. J. Gergen (Eds.), *The self in social interaction.* Vol. 1. New York: Wiley, 1968.

Baldwin, J. M. *Social and ethical interpretations in mental development.* New York: Macmillan, 1897.

Bateson, G., Jackson, D. D., Haley, J., & Weakland, J. H. Toward a theory of schizophrenia. *Behavioral Science,* 1956, **1,** 251–256.

Bergin, A. E. The effect of dissonant persuasive communications upon changes in self-referring attitudes. *Journal of Personality,* 1962, **30,** 423–438.

Berkeley, G. A. *A treatise concerning the principles of human knowledge.* (Reprinted) Oxford: Claredon Press, 1901.

Berscheid, E., & Walster, E. H. *Interpersonal attraction.* Reading, Mass.: Addison-Wesley, 1969.

Bertocci, P. A. The psychological self, the ego and personality. *Psychological Review,* 1945, **52,** 91–99 (A philosopher's attempt to deal with critical issues raised in Part II).

95

Blau, P. M. *Exchange and power in social life.* New York: Wiley, 1964.

Block, J. The assessment of communication: Role variations as a function of interactional context. *Journal of Personality,* 1952, **21,** 272–286.

Brehm, J. W. A dissonance analysis of attitude-discrepant behavior. In C. I. Hovland & M. J. Rosenberg (Eds.), *Attitude organization and change.* New Haven, Conn.: Yale University Press, 1960.

Brehm, J. W., & Cohen, A. R. *Explorations in cognitive dissonance.* New York: Wiley, 1962.

Brown, R. *Words and things.* New York: Free Press, 1958. (A detailed discussion of language and its relationship to concepts.)

Brown, R. *Social psychology.* New York: Free Press, 1965. (An excellent discussion in brief of language and concept formation on pp. 246–349.)

Bruner, J. S. On perceptual readiness. *Psychological Review,* 1957, **64,** 123–152. (A classic discussion of conceptual process and its function.)

Bruner, J. S., Goodnow, J. J., & Austin, G. A. *A study of thinking.* New York: Wiley, 1956. (Detailed studies of concept formation.)

Calkins, M. W. The self in recent psychology. *Psychological Bulletin,* 1912, **9,** 25–30.

Canon, L. K. Self-confidence and selective exposure to information. In L. Festinger, *Conflict, decision and dissonance.* Stanford, Calif.: Stanford University Press, 1964.

Carlsmith, J. M., Collins, B. E., & Helmreich, R. K. Studies in forced compliance; I. The effect of pressure for compliance on attitude change produced by face-to-face role playing and anonymous essay writing. *Journal of Personality and Social Psychology,* 1966, **4,** 1–13.

Cohen, A. R. Experimental effects of ego-defense preference on interpersonal relations. *Journal of Abnormal and Social Psychology,* 1956, **52,** 19–27.

Cohen, A. R. Some implications of self-esteem for social influence. In C. I. Hovland, & I. L. Janis (Eds.), *Personality and persuasibility.* New Haven, Conn.: Yale University Press, 1959.

Cooley, C. H. *Human nature and the social order.* New York: Scribner, 1922.

Coopersmith, S. *The antecedents of self-esteem.* San Francisco: Freeman, 1967.

Cox, D. B., & Bauer, R. A. Self-confidence and persuasibility in women. *Public Opinion Quarterly,* 1964, **28,** 453–466.

Crowne, D. P., & Marlowe, D. *The approval motive; studies in evaluative dependence.* New York: Wiley, 1964.

Descartes, R. *Principles of philosophy.* (Reprinted) New York: Dover Press, 1955.

Deutsch, M., & Solomon, L. Reactions to evaluations by others as influenced by self evaluations. *Sociometry,* 1959, **22,** 93–112.

Dickoff, H. Reactions to evaluations by another person as a function of self evaluation and the interaction context. Unpublished doctoral dissertation, Duke University, 1961.

Diggory, J. C. *Self-evaluation: concepts and studies.* New York: Wiley, 1966 (Ch. 1–3 examine traditional issues of self-conception in detail).

Diggory, J. C., Klein, S. J., & Cohen, N. M. Muscle-action potentials and estimated probability of success. *Journal of Experimental Psychology*, 1964, **68**, 448–456.

Elms, A. C. (Ed.) *Role playing, reward and attitude change.* Princeton, N.J.: Van Nostrand, 1969.

Eriksen, C. W., & Browne, C. T. An experimental and theoretical analysis of perceptual defense. *Journal of Abnormal and Social Psychology*, 1956, **52**, 224–230.

Erikson, E. H. The problem of ego identity. *Psychological issues*, 1959, **1**, 101–166.

Festinger, L. A theory of social comparison. *Human Relations*, 1954, **14**, 48–64.

Festinger, L. *A theory of cognitive dissonance.* Evanston, Ill.: Row, Peterson & Company, 1957.

Festinger, L., & Carlsmith, J. M. Cognitive consequences of forced compliance. *Journal of Abnormal and Social Psychology*, 1959, **58**, 203–210.

Freud, S. *A general introduction to psychoanalysis.* New York: Buni and Liveright, 1920.

Fromm, E. Selfishness and self love. *Psychiatry*, 1939, **2**, 507–523. (Also reprinted in Gordon & Gergen.)

Gergen, K. J. Interaction goals and personalistic feedback as factors affecting the presentation of self. *Journal of Personality and Social Psychology*, 1965, **1**, 413–424.

Gergen, K. J. The significance of skin color in human relations. *Daedalus*, Spring, 1967, 390–406.

Gergen, K. J. Personal consistency and the presentation of self. In Gordon & Gergen.

Gergen, K. J. Self theory and the process of self-observation. *Journal of Nervous and Mental Disease*, 1969, **148**, 437–448.

Gergen, K. J. Perception of others and the self. In K. Back (Ed.), *Basic issues in social psychology.* New York: Wiley, in press.

Gergen, K. J. & Bauer, R. A. The interactive effects of self-esteem and task difficulty on social conformity. *Journal of Personality and Social Psychology*, 1967, **6**, 16–22.

Gergen, K. J., & Morse, S. J. Self-consistency: Measurement and validation. *Proceedings of the American Psychological Association*, 1967, 207–208.

Gergen, K. J., & Taylor, M. G. Role playing and modifying the self-concept. Paper presented at the Meetings of the Eastern Psychological Association, March, 1966, New York.

Gergen, K. J., & Taylor, M. G. Social expectancy and self-presentation in a status hierarchy. *Journal of Experimental Social Psychology*, 1969, **5**, 79–92.

Gergen, K. J., & Wishnov, B. Others' self evaluations and interaction anticipation as determinants of self presentation. *Journal of Personality and Social Psychology*, 1965, **2**, 348–358.

Goffman, E. *The presentation of self in everyday life.* New York: Doubleday, 1959.

Goffman, E. *Asylums.* New York: Doubleday, 1961.

Gordon, C. Self-conceptions: Configurations of content. In Gordon & Gergen.

Gordon, C., & Gergen, K. J. (Eds.) *The self in social interaction.* Vol. 1. New York: Wiley, 1968. (Contains classic readings on self along with contemporary research findings.)

Gore, P. M., & Rotter, J. B. A personality correlate of social action. *Journal of Personality,* 1963, **31**, 58–64.

Hartshorne, H., & May, M. A. *Studies in deceit.* New York: Macmillan, 1928.

Hastorf, A. The creation of group leaders. In K. J. Gergen & D. Marlowe (Eds.), *Personality and Social Behavior.* Reading, Mass.: Addison Wesley, 1970.

Hobbes, T. *Leviathan.* (Reprinted) London: Andrew Crooke, 1946.

Horney, K. *Neurosis and human growth.* New York: Norton, 1950. (See especially pp. 155–174; reprinted in Gordon & Gergen.)

Hume, D. *Treatise on human nature.* Oxford: Clarendon Press, 1888.

James, W. *Principles of psychology.* New York: Holt, 1892.

James, W. *Psychology: the briefer course.* New York: Holt, 1910. (See especially pp. 177 and following.)

Janis, I. L., & King, B. T. The influence of role-playing on opinion change. *Journal of Abnormal and Social Psychology,* 1954, **49**, 211–218.

Janis, I. L., & Mann, L. Effectiveness of emotional role-playing in modifying smoking habits and attitudes. *Journal of Experimental Research in Personality,* 1965, **1**, 84–90.

Jansen, M. J., & Stolurow, L. M. An experimental study of role playing. *Psychological Monographs,* 1962, **76** (Whole No. 550).

Jaspers, K. *Being and time.* (Reprinted) New York: Meridian, 1957.

Jones, E. E., & Aneshansel, J. The learning and utilization of contravaluant material. *Journal of Abnormal and Social Psychology,* 1956, **53**, 27–34.

Jones, E. E., Gergen, K. J., & Davis, K. Some reactions to being approved or disapproved as a person. *Psychological Monographs,* 1962, **76,** (whole No. 521).

Jones, E. E., Gergen, K. J., & Jones, R. G. Tactics of ingratiation among leaders and subordinates in a status hierarchy. *Psychological Monographs,* 1963, **77** (Whole No. 566).

Jourard, S. *The transparent self.* Princeton, N.J.: Van Nostrand Insight, 1964. (Essays on the importance to mental health of disclosing oneself to others.)

Jung, C. G. *Two essays on analytical psychology.* New York: Dodd, Mead, 1928.

Kardiner, A., & Ovesey, L. *The mark of oppression.* New York: World Publishing, 1951. (An analytic account of self-esteem and the American Negro. See especially pp. 302–317; reprinted in Gordon & Gergen.)

Kelly, G. A. *The Psychology of Personal Constructs.* New York: Norton, 1955.

Kierkegaard, S. *Sickness unto death.* (Reprinted) New York: Doubleday, 1955.

Kiesler, S. B., & Baral, R. L. The search for a romantic partner: The effects of self-esteem and physical attractiveness on romantic behavior. In K. J. Gergen, & D. Marlowe (Eds.), *Personality and social behavior.* Reading, Mass.: Addison-Wesley, 1970.

Lecky, P. *Self-consistency: A theory of personality.* Long Island, N.Y.: The Island Press, 1945. (A theory of personality based on the self-consistency assumption.)

Lee, Dorothy. *Freedom and culture.* New York: Prentice-Hall, 1959 (see pp. 131–140).

Lesser, G., & Abelson, R. Correlates of persuasibility in children. In C. I. Hovland & I. L. Janis (Eds.), *Personality and Persuasibility.* New Haven: Yale University Press, 1959.

Levine, J. M., & Murphy, G. The learning and forgetting of controversial material. *Journal of Abnormal and Social Psychology,* 1943, **38,** 507–517.

Lewin, K. *Principles of topological psychology.* New York: McGraw-Hill, 1936.

Ludwig, A. M. *The importance of lying.* Springfield, Ill.: Charles C Thomas, 1965 (An examination of the positive effects of duplicity and inconsistency).

Lynd, H. M. *On shame and the search for identity.* New York: Wiley, 1961. (See especially pp. 226–245, reprinted in Gordon & Gergen.)

Mead, G. H. *Mind, self and society.* Chicago: University of Chicago Press, 1934.

Merton, R. K. Bureaucratic structure and personality. *Social Forces.* 1940, **57,** 560–568.

Mill, J. *Analysis of the Phenomena of the Human Mind.* (Reprinted) London: Longmans, 1869.

Mill, J. S. *An examination of Sir William Hamilton's philosophy.* London: Longmans, 1865.

Morse, S. J., & Gergen, K. J. Social comparison, self-consistency and the concept of self. *Journal of Personality and Social Psychology,* in press.

Pepitone, A. Motivational effects in social perception. *Human Relations,* 1950, **1,** 57–76.

Pepitone, A. Some conceptual and empirical problems of consistency models. In S. Feldman (Ed.), *Cognitive Consistency.* New York: Academic Press, 1967.

Rogers, C. Therapy, personality and interpersonal relationships. In S. Koch (Ed.), *Psychology: A study of a science.* Vol. III. New York: McGraw-Hill, 1959. (Outstanding statement of relationship between self-regard and mental disorder.)

Rogers, C. *On becoming a person.* Boston: Houghton Mifflin, 1961.

Rosen, A. C. Change in perceptual threshold as a protective function of the organism. *Journal of Personality,* 1954, **23,** 182–195.

Rosenberg, M. *Society and the adolescent self-image.* Princeton, N.J.: Princeton University Press, 1965.

Rosenberg, M. J. When dissonance fails: On eliminating evaluation apprehension from attitude measurement. *Journal of Personality and Social Psychology*, 1965, **1**, 28–43.

Sansom, E. *The perfect gentleman*. London: Heath, 1956.

Sarbin, T. R. A preface to a psychological analysis of the self. *Psychological Review*, 1952, **59**, 11–22. (A detailed examination of self-development from a cognitive viewpoint; reprinted in Gordon & Gergen.)

Schachter, S. The interaction of cognitive and physiological determinants of emotional state. In L. Berkowitz (Ed.), *Advances in experimental social psychology*. Vol. 1. New York: Academic Press, 1964.

Scott, W. A. Attitude changes by response reinforcement: Replication and extension. *Sociometry*, 1959, **22**, 328–335.

Skinner, B. F. *The behavior of organisms: An experimental analysis*. New York: Appleton, 1938.

Strauss, A. L. *Mirrors and Masks: The search for identity*. Glencoe, Ill.: Free Press, 1959. (A lively account of the relationship between roles and identity.)

Sullivan, H. S. *The interpersonal theory of psychiatry*. New York: Norton, 1953. (See especially pp. 158 and following.)

Taft, R. Selective recall and memory distortion of favorable and unfavorable material. *Journal of Abnormal and Social Psychology*, 1954, **49**, 23–29.

Thomas, R., & Burdick, R. Self-esteem and inter-personal influence. *Journal of Personality and Social Psychology*, 1954, **51**, 419–426.

Tiryakian, E. A. The existential self and the person. In Gordon & Gergen. (A sensitive treatment of the relationship of self to existential concerns.)

Titchener, E. B. A note on the consciousness of self. *American Journal of Psychology*, 1911, **22**, 540–552. (An early statement by an outstanding perceptual psychologist.)

Turner, R. H. The self-conception in social interaction. In Gordon & Gergen. (Good integrative discussion of development and function of self-conception.)

Veblen, T. *The theory of the leisure class*. (Reprinted) New York: Mentor Books, 1958. (See especially pp. 37–40; reprinted in Gordon & Gergen.)

Videbeck, R. Self-conception and the reaction of others. *Sociometry*, 1960, **23**, 351–362.

Waller, W. *The sociology of teaching*. New York: Wiley, 1932.

Walster, E. The effect of self-esteem on romantic liking. *Journal of Experimental Social Psychology*, 1965, **1**, 184–197.

Weinstein, A. *Altercasting and interpersonal relations*. In P. Secord & C. Backman (Eds.), *Readings in Social Psychology*. New York: Prentice-Hall, 1967.

Weiss, P. Self-alienation and psychiatry today. *American Journal of Psychiatry*, 1961, **28**, 206–217.

Wheelis, A. *The quest for identity.* New York: Norton, 1958 (Problems of identity are contrasted with neurosis from the psychoanalytic viewpoint).

Whorf, B. L. *Language, thought and reality.* J. B. Carroll (Ed.) New York: Wiley, 1956. (Classic discussion of thought and language in cross-cultural perspective.)

Williams, T. *The Roman spring of Mrs. Stone.* New York: Atheneum, 1958.

Wylie, R. *The self concept.* Lincoln, Nebr.: University of Nebraska Press, 1961. (A thorough critique of early research on self-conception.)

Zimbardo, P. G. The effect of effort and improvisation on self-persuasion produced by role-playing. *Journal of Experimental Social Psychology,* 1965, **1,** 103–120.

AUTHOR INDEX

SUBJECT INDEX

NOTES

NOTES

NOTES

NOTES

NOTES

NOTES